OECD Public Governance Reviews

I0120177

OECD Integrity Review of Thailand 2021

ACHIEVING EFFECTIVE INTEGRITY POLICIES AND SUSTAINED REFORM

OECD
BETTER POLICIES FOR BETTER LIVES

This document, as well as any data and map included herein, are without prejudice to the status of or sovereignty over any territory, to the delimitation of international frontiers and boundaries and to the name of any territory, city or area.

The statistical data for Israel are supplied by and under the responsibility of the relevant Israeli authorities. The use of such data by the OECD is without prejudice to the status of the Golan Heights, East Jerusalem and Israeli settlements in the West Bank under the terms of international law.

Please cite this publication as:
OECD (2021), *OECD Integrity Review of Thailand 2021: Achieving Effective Integrity Policies and Sustained Reform*, OECD Public Governance Reviews, OECD Publishing, Paris, *https://doi.org/10.1787/e8949f1b-en*.

ISBN 978-92-64-59351-0 (print)
ISBN 978-92-64-57642-1 (pdf)

OECD Public Governance Reviews
ISSN 2219-0406 (print)
ISSN 2219-0414 (online)

Foreword

With the achievement of the OECD Integrity Review of Thailand 2021 – Phase 2, Thailand has become the first country in Asia-Pacific completing a full review of the key pillars of the country's public integrity system. This demonstrates the Government of Thailand's continued commitment to investing in public integrity and sharing practices and expertise with OECD countries. The Review was conducted by the Directorate for Public Governance through a series of consultations with the Thai stakeholders, and is part of the Thailand-OECD Country Programme and the Directorate's broader work programme on public sector integrity. Tackling corruption in the public sector and building transparent and accountable public institutions fosters investment, encourages competition, and improves government efficiency. The policy recommendations in this Integrity Review not only seek to bolster Thailand's integrity system, but also to promote public trust and ensure that the country can continue down a path of sustained economic growth.

In recent years, the Government of Thailand has continued to strengthen efforts to mitigate corruption risks in the public sector and to implement the 20-year Anti-Corruption Master Plan (2017-2036), guided by the 20-year National Strategy (2018-2037), the National Anti-Corruption Strategy, Phase Three (2017-2021), and the 12th National Economic and Social Development Plan (2017-2021). Moreover, in follow-up of the recommendations of OECD Integrity Review of Thailand – Phase 1, Thailand has recently improved its institutional co-ordination and measurement frameworks on corruption prevention and has streamlined the institutional mandates for corruption investigations.

This Integrity Review – Phase 2 deepens the analysis on three key elements of Thailand's integrity system, namely disciplinary mechanisms and sanctions, risk management, and integrity in policy and decision making in the public sector. It provides recommendations in line with international good practices and the 2017 OECD Recommendation of the Council on Public Integrity, such as ensuring coherence in its disciplinary processes, strengthening corruption risk management practices, and improving the regulatory framework for interactions between public and private sectors.

Under the direction and oversight of Elsa Pilichowski, Director for Public Governance, and Julio Bacio Terracino, Acting Head of the Public Sector Integrity Division, this review was co-ordinated by Jeroen Michels, and the chapters have been written by Jeroen Michels, Pelagia Patsoule, Mariana Prats, and Gavin Ugale. The report greatly benefitted from the insights and comments from Julio Bacio Terracino, Frédéric Boehm, Pauline Bertrand, and Jelena Damnjanovic. The review was prepared for publication by Meral Gedik, Balazs Gyimesi and Andrea Uhrhammer. Aleksandra Bogusz, Jelena Damnjanovic, Rania Haidar, and Charles Victor provided valuable administrative assistance.

The OECD expresses its gratitude to the Government of Thailand, and in particular, to the Office of Public Sector Development Commission (OPDC) and the Office of the Public Sector Anti-Corruption Commission (PACC) for their support and inputs throughout the project. This review also significantly benefited from the comments provided by the Office of the Civil Service Commission (OCSC), the Office of the Auditor General, and the Secretariat of the Cabinet. Particular appreciation goes to all the participants who actively engaged in debates and provided valuable insights during the fact-finding mission in Bangkok on 11-13 December 2019. This review also benefitted from the valuable input of the officials from OPDC, PACC, and the Secretariat of the Cabinet during their time at the OECD on the secondment programme in 2020.

This document was approved by the OECD Working Party of Senior Public Integrity Officials (SPIO) on 21 April 2021 and declassified by the Public Governance Committee on 21 May 2021. It was prepared for publication by the OECD Secretariat.

Table of contents

FIGURES

TABLES

Follow OECD Publications on:

http://twitter.com/OECD_Pubs

http://www.facebook.com/OECDPublications

http://www.linkedin.com/groups/OECD-Publications-4645871

http://www.youtube.com/oecdilibrary

http://www.oecd.org/oecddirect/

Executive summary

A sound public integrity system requires a multi-faceted approach, in which disciplinary mechanisms and sanctions, risk management, and integrity in policy and decision making play a pivotal role. Enforcing the integrity measures through sanctions is a necessary element to prevent impunity among public officials and to ensure the credibility of the integrity system as a whole. Integrity risk management supports decision making and ultimately helps to ensure the achievement of integrity objectives. Integrity in decision making ensures the pursuit of the public interest in policy making and improves the delivery of public services in the long-term, promotes fair competition and helps restore trust in government. The Integrity Review of Thailand – Phase 2 deepens the analysis in these three key areas of Thailand's integrity system, in line with the 2017 OECD Recommendation of the Council on Public Integrity. Together with the OECD Integrity Review of Thailand – Phase 1, the finalisation of this Phase 2 makes Thailand the first country in Asia-Pacificto complete a full review of the key pillars of the country's public integrity system.

Regarding disciplinary mechanisms, Thailand has a solid foundation in place for enforcing integrity rules and standards as stipulated in the Civil Service Act B.E. 2551 (2008), which covers the disciplinary regime for officials hired and appointed to government service. However, further reforms are required to improve its quality and introduce a more coherent approach to disciplinary processes.

In order to strengthen the quality of the disciplinary investigations, the Office of the Public Sector Anti-Corruption Commission (PACC) and the Office of the Civil Service Commission (OCSC) may establish a registry of trained disciplinary investigators with appropriate legal and investigative background and create "shared" disciplinary offices. PACC and OCSC may also establish fixed timeframes for the conclusion of each step of the disciplinary investigation to ensure timeliness and efficiency. As multiple institutions currently hold similar roles for disciplinary investigations, Thailand may reduce complexity in the institutional set-up by centralising the mandate for carrying out disciplinary investigations under PACC. Furthermore, although efforts have been made to collect data on the disciplinary system, there is currently no systematic approach for using disciplinary data to improve integrity policies. In response, Thailand may centralise the responsibility for collecting and processing statistical disciplinary data to the OCSC, make selected disciplinary information publicly accessible, and leverage collected data to assess the effectiveness of the disciplinary enforcement system

Risk management is another key pillar for a sound integrity system and good governance. Recent national reforms in Thailand have helped to modernise the government's approach to identifying and responding to risks. Nonetheless, key areas for improvement remain. First, the Thai government, particularly the Comptroller General's Department (CGD), can further clarify the roles and responsibilities for managing risks in its own policies and guidelines. This also can be an opportunity to further refine the CGD's communications strategies to promote the value of risk management as a management tool for better decision making and good governance, rather than a compliance exercise. Second, the government can improve its strategy for and implementation of integrity risk assessments. The OECD identified at least three different approaches to assessing risks, which are carried out by different entities in government. Harmonising these efforts can help to reduce potential duplication and ensure government officials understand their obligations for managing risks and controls. Capacity building with regards to assessing risks, especially at the regional level, is also a critical area for improvement. Lastly, there are opportunities to ensure continuous improvements to integrity risk management and the maturation of the internal control system as a whole. Monitoring and evaluation (M&E) policies and practices are critical elements of an internal control policy, as reflected in international standards. The CGD can further develop M&E plans, as well as a process for quality assurance assessments, to advance learning and ongoing improvement.

Regarding integrity in policy design and decision making in the public sector, the enactment of the Act on Legislative Drafting and Evaluation of Legislation B.E. 2560 (2019) was a considerable step towards promoting integrity in decision-making processes. The Act requires to involve the public throughout the entire drafting process, and, additionally, it establishes the need to develop a centralised system, providing details and guidance on processes and gathering all information on public consultations. This promotes stakeholder engagement and participation, as well as the effective enforcement of the regulation.

Despite this advance, there remains a lack of specific regulations on interaction between the private and the public sector during legislative drafting or policy making process more broadly, as well as a lack of public information on policy makers' agendas or composition of committees. This regulatory shortfall makes Thailand's public policies vulnerable to capture by special interests. This is confirmed by the World Economic Forum's Global Competitiveness Report 2017-2018, showing that Thailand exhibits lower levels of perceived transparency in government policy making than other countries in Southeast Asia and the OECD. At the same time, according to the Global Right to Information Index (RTI) the legal quality of Thailand's Official Information Act is slightly above the average score of other South East Asia countries. Building on this, it is vital that the upcoming reform of the Official Information Act B.E 2540 (1997) provides guidance for citizens on how to request information and strengthens the independence of the Information Commissioner by, for example, making its decisions binding and providing it with its own budget.

1 Ensuring a fair, effective and coherent disciplinary system for public officials in Thailand

This chapter reviews the disciplinary system for public officials in Thailand, with particular attention to fairness, policy coherence, institutional co-ordination and the use of data. Although Thailand has a solid foundation for enforcing integrity rules and standards, further reforms are required to improve its quality and introduce a more coherent approach to disciplinary processes. For example, Thailand may strengthen the corps of disciplinary investigators and leverage the use of data on sanctions.

Introduction

A comprehensive and advanced integrity framework seeking to curb corruption successfully cannot only rely on prevention and detection but should also invest efforts in developing an effective enforcement mechanism. Enforcing the integrity rules and standards is a necessary element to prevent impunity among public officials and to ensure the credibility of the integrity system as a whole. Effective responses to integrity violations, and the application of sanctions in a fair, objective and timely manner help ensure accountability and build the necessary legitimacy for integrity rules and frameworks to deter people from carrying out misconducts. Furthermore, a consistent application of rules within the public sector is an important message to citizens, which can inspire confidence in the government's ability to tackle corruption effectively and defend the public interest.

This chapter examines the role and effectiveness of the disciplinary system in Thailand as a key mechanism for enforcing public integrity standards. Drawing from international standards and norms, as well as international good practices, the chapter assesses the strengths and weaknesses of the current framework. The assessment is centred around the OECD Recommendation on Public Integrity (OECD, 2017[1]) calling States to ensure that enforcement mechanisms – including disciplinary ones – provide appropriate responses to all suspected violations of public integrity standards by public officials. In light of this framework, the analysis focuses on:

- the extent to which integrity rules are applied fairly, objectively and timely among Thailand's public officials
- whether mechanisms for co-operation and exchange of information are effectively in place among all relevant institutions (i.e disciplinary departments of government agencies, the OCSC, the PACC, the NACC, the Police and the Public Prosecutor)
- how the disciplinary system of Thailand collects data, ensures its transparency and evaluates its performance.

Overview of disciplinary proceedings for public officials in Thailand

Public officials in Thailand are subject to different disciplinary regimes depending on their category. Specific procedures apply to police,[1] military, prosecutors and judges,[2] as well as for elected officials. The disciplinary regime for the majority of public officials not falling under these categories is determined in the Civil Service Act B.E. 2551 (2008), which covers officials hired and appointed to government service under its provisions. As far as local government officials are concerned, there is a specific law[3] in place, however the disciplinary process is similar to the one described in the Civil Service Act.

Misconducts of public officials are usually identified through relevant allegations, which are received by different entry points. Investigations can be carried out by a multitude of actors with different responsibilities (see Table 1.1), depending on the entity receiving the allegation.

Table 1.1. Key actors of the disciplinary system in Thailand and their responsibilities

	Actor	Type of agency	Responsibilities	Legal framework
Policy design and implementation	Civil Service Commission	Statutory Board	• Makes proposals and advises the Cabinet on policies and strategies regarding human resource management in the public sector • Prescribes rules, directives regulations and guidelines for administration of human resource management in government agencies and other issues imposed by the Civil Service Act and related laws	Civil Service Act, B.E. 2551 (2008)
Policy design and implementation	Office of the Civil Service Commission (OCSC)	Government agency reporting to the Prime Minister	• Central agency for human resource (HR) standards, including civil service ethics, disciplinary enforcement, complaint handling, Code of Conduct for civil servants • Responsible for developing laws and policies related to disciplinary enforcement • Develops training and standards for disciplinary proceedings	Civil Service Act, B.E.2551 (2008)
Investigations	National Anti-Corruption Commission (NACC)	Constitutionally independent agency	• Carries out investigations related to the misconduct of public officials upon receiving relevant allegations • Exclusively responsible for carrying out investigations related to serious corruption offences	Organic Act on Counter Corruption, B.E. 2561 (2018)
Investigations	Office of the Public Sector Anti-Corruption Commission (PACC)	Government agency part of the executive branch, reporting to the Prime Minister	• Carries out investigations related to the misconduct of public officials • Investigations are carried out either upon receiving a relevant allegation or upon assignment from the NACC • Reports the result of the investigations to the Public Sector Anti-Corruption Commission according to the Executive Measures in Anti-Corruption Act, B.E. 2551 (2008) and the additional amendment	Executive Measures in Anti-Corruption Act, B.E. 2551 (2008) (and the additional amendment)
Investigations and imposition of sanctions	Government entities	Government agencies part of the executive branch	• Heads of government entities ("supervising officials") are responsible for disciplinary enforcement • Upon receiving relevant allegations, a commission of inquiry is appointed to carry out the investigation • Head of government entity ("supervising official") examines the investigation findings and decides whether to impose a sanction or not	Civil Service Act, B.E.2551 (2008)
Appeals	Merit System Protection Commission (MSPC)	Quasi-judicial body	• Considers appeals submitted by public officials regarding disciplinary procedures affecting them; • Reviews the merit of departments' rules and regulations	Civil Service Act, B.E.2551 (2008)
Appeals	Administrative Court of First Instance	Judicial court	• Decides over appeals of MSPC rulings about complaints related to the treatment of civil servants by supervising officials.	Civil Service Act, B.E.2551 (2008) Act on Establishment of the Administrative Court and Administrative Court Procedure, B.E. 2542 (1999)
Appeals	Supreme Administrative Court	Judicial court	• Decides over appeals of MSPC rulings related to the imposition of disciplinary sanctions.	Civil Service Act, B.E.2551 (2008) Act on Establishment of the Administrative Court and Administrative Court Procedure, B.E. 2542 (1999)

Source: Developed by OECD.

The disciplinary process takes place within the government entities and follows the provisions of the Civil Service Act, B.E. 2551 (2008). Disciplinary offences are usually identified through complaints, discovery by the supervising official or investigations carried out by other institutions, such as the NACC and the PACC. Once a complaint is received or a misconduct is otherwise identified, the supervising official[4] launches a preliminary investigation to determine whether the case has merit or not. The supervising official may undertake the preliminary investigation himself/herself, or assign a civil servant or relevant state official to undertake the preliminary investigation and file a report for taking into consideration (see Box 1.1). If there are reasonable grounds to move forward with the investigation of the case, the supervising official classifies the alleged misconduct as a serious or non-serious disciplinary offence, otherwise the case is dismissed.

Box 1.1. Stages and procedures of the disciplinary process within government agencies

The disciplinary process aims to collect evidence regarding the factual truth of an allegation. To that end, the commission of inquiry carries out the disciplinary investigation applying the principles of justice, fairness and timeliness through the following procedural steps:

1. Determination of approaches and points of investigation.
2. Notification of the accused person and explanation of allegation.
3. Asking the accused person whether he/she wishes to admit or deny.
4. Taking evidence from the party making the allegation.
5. Notifying the accused person of the summary of evidence in support of the allegation.
6. Interrogating the accused person.
7. Taking evidence from the accused person.
8. Examination of evidence from both sides and forming an opinion.
9. Preparation of an investigation report.

Source: (OCSC, 2014[2]).

Once the investigation is completed, the commission summarises its findings and gathered evidence and shares it in a report with the supervising official. As a minimum, the investigation report includes the following information:

- summary of facts and evidence
- weighing of evidence
- opinion of the commission of inquiry.

As a final step, the supervising official decides whether to proceed with the imposition of a sanction or not. It should be noted that disciplinary sanctions can only be imposed by the respective government agency. An officer found guilty of a breach can lodge a complaint with the Merit System Protection Commission (MSPC) in order to appeal against the verdict. The MSPC carries out the appeal consideration or may appoint an appeals commission to examine the appeal. The ruling of the MSPC is binding for the supervising official. In case the public official disagrees with the MSPC ruling, a complaint can be filed at the Supreme Administrative Court, which is responsible for the final decision.

In light of this overview, the following section focuses on the mechanisms Thailand has in place for ensuring the fairness, objectivity and timeliness of disciplinary proceedings, as well as the co-operation, exchange of information and transparency within the disciplinary regime and across enforcement mechanisms.

Ensuring fairness, objectivity and timeliness

The types and classification of disciplinary breaches are clearly defined, supporting consistent application of the legal framework

The OECD Recommendation stresses the need for fairness, objectivity and timeliness in the enforcement of public integrity standards, calling on countries to apply these key principles in all relevant enforcement regimes. These three elements contribute to building or restoring the public's trust in standards and enforcement mechanisms, and are applied both at the level of investigations, as well as at the level of court proceedings and imposition of sanctions.

In Thailand, the Civil Service Act establishes the obligations for public servants and the competent authorities to address misconduct through disciplinary proceedings. Furthermore, the act establishes sanctions for public servants who commit disciplinary offences, which are distinguished between "serious breaches of discipline and "non-serious breaches of discipline". As highlighted in Table 1.2, the classification of the offence affects the sanction imposed. Serious breaches of discipline cover mostly different types of fraud (i.e. false claims for stipends and official travel allowances, providing undue, etc.) and other criminal offences (e.g. gambling, consumption of intoxicating substances).

Table 1.2. Typology of misconducts and sanctions in Thailand

Type of misconduct	Type of sanction
Non-serious disciplinary breach	Depending on the case: • written reprimand • salary deduction • salary reduction Alternatively: Written parole or admonishment when there are reasons to refrain from punishment.
Serious disciplinary breach	• Dismissal • Expulsion depending on the gravity of the case

Source: Elaborated by OECD based on materials provided.

Thailand's sanctioning regime is quite comprehensive compared to other countries (see Box 1.2) covering different types of sanctions of administrative nature.

Box 1.2. Administrative disciplinary sanctions in selected OECD member and partner countries

OECD member and partner countries provide for these and additional types of sanctions including:

- Fines.
- Demotion in rank (France, Germany, Spain, and the United States).
- Salary reduction (Germany, the Netherlands) or withholding of future periodic salary increases (the Netherlands, United Kingdom).
- Compulsory transfer with obligation to change residence (France, Spain, United Kingdom).
- Compulsory retirement (France).
- Reduction or loss of pension rights (Germany – for retired officials, and Brazil).
- Reduction in right to holiday or personal leave (the Netherlands).

Sources: (OECD, 2017[3]); (Cardona, 2003[4]).

The Civil Service Act clearly sets the definition on "non-serious breaches of discipline" (Section 84) and also stipulates what consists of a "serious breach of discipline" (Section 85). Moreover, the OCSC manual on disciplinary proceedings (OCSC, 2014[2]) provides helpful examples and descriptions of what constitutes a serious breach of discipline, further supporting the consistent application of the legal framework.

Furthermore, Section 42 (4) of the Civil Service Act underlines that disciplinary proceedings must be carried out justly and without prejudice. As such, the supervising official has to take into account the merit-based principle in every step of the disciplinary procedure, including the imposition of sanctions.

In terms of checks and balances, Section 103 of the Civil Service Act further states that, after a supervising official has ordered punishment, a report shall be submitted to the Ministerial Civil Service Sub-Commission or to the CSC. In the case where the Ministerial Civil Service Sub-Commission or the CSC finds that the disciplinary proceeding has not been correct or appropriate, the supervising official can be ordered to implement a correcting resolution by the Ministerial Civil Service Sub-Commission or the CSC, a mechanism further ensuring consistent application of the law.

Additional safeguards are needed to strengthen the integrity of supervising officials and ensure the fair imposition of sanctions

Disciplinary actions should only be taken based on the law and those enforcing the law should therefore act objectively. Objectivity should apply through all the phases of relevant proceedings. This might prove challenging in the disciplinary regime, where decisions – at least at the first instance level – are usually taken by quasi-judicial bodies, which are administrative in nature and do not enjoy same procedural guaranties as judicial authorities.

In Thailand, disciplinary decisions are taken by the supervising official in charge of hiring public officials according to Sections 57 and 90 of the Civil Service Act. This is usually the head of the government entity, who is responsible for the following:

- Determining the merit of the case and the nature of the disciplinary offence at the level of the preliminary investigation.
- Appointing the commission of inquiry responsible for conducting the formal disciplinary investigation.
- Deciding about the possible imposition of sanctions.

In the case of a non-serious breach of discipline, section 92 of the Civil Service Act provides that the supervising official may initiate disciplinary proceedings without any further procedural requirements. To notify the accused public official, a written record of the allegation ("statement of alleged wrongdoing") is served stating the breach of discipline examined. In the case of an allegation of a serious breach of discipline, section 93 provides that a commission of inquiry must be appointed. Such an appointment of a commission of inquiry is considered a "statement of alleged wrongdoing" and is shared with the accused person to notify him or her about the alleged wrongdoing.

While the supervising official has wide discretionary powers, there are several checks and balances in place to ensure the integrity of the disciplinary process. First of all, the accused person can object to the composition of the inquiry commission if, for example, there is a personal involvement or connection with any of the commissioners or other causes that would prevent impartiality. Secondly, the public official sanctioned has the right to appeal the decision of the supervising official at two stages – first at the MSPC and then at the Administrative Court. Moreover, principles and guarantees of fairness are mentioned extensively in the OCSC Manual for Disciplinary Proceedings with the rule of law and the obligation to reach the truth of facts and reaching decisions with equality and without any favouritism being the key elements (OCSC, 2014[2]).

Despite these checks and balances, challenges remain in practice in ensuring the integrity of the supervising official and the objectivity of decisions taken. Indeed, interviews with Thai stakeholders have indicated that the decision-making process is rather discretionary. To that end, procedural safeguards should be in place to guarantee that disciplinary actions are free from internal or external influence, as well as any form of conflict of interest.

As a minimum, these procedural safeguards can include the following components:

- Ensuring that personnel responsible for disciplinary proceedings are selected based on objective, merit-based criteria (particularly senior-level positions).
- Ensuring personnel responsible for disciplinary proceedings enjoy an appropriate level of job security and competitive salaries *vis-à-vis* their job requirement.
- Ensuring personnel responsible for disciplinary proceedings are protected from threats and duress so as to not fear reprisal.
- Ensuring personnel responsible for disciplinary proceedings have autonomy in the selection of cases to take forward.
- Ensuring personnel responsible for disciplinary proceedings receive timely training on conflict-of-interest situations and have clear procedures for managing them (OECD, 2017[3]).

Establishing registries of trained disciplinary investigators or piloting "shared" disciplinary services would help improve the quality of disciplinary investigations

The commission of inquiry is the main investigatory body for disciplinary cases in government agencies and is responsible for gathering evidence with the purpose of verifying the facts and ensuring justice (see Box 1.1). The disciplinary investigation differs from the criminal procedure, which focuses on gathering evidence to support the prosecution's allegation with less regard given to the evidence provided by the suspect or witnesses.

In carrying out disciplinary investigations, the members of the commission of inquiry are considered investigative officers under the Criminal Code with the duty to report facts, exercise discretion in determining the facts of the case, as well as in advising supervising officials on the imposition of sanctions. The main purpose of the commission of inquiry is to obtain factual proof with an obligation to hear both sides of an allegation. It is composed of at least three members: a chairman and two other commissioners. One commissioner is designated as the secretary. In the interest of the inquiry, there may be an assistant secretary. The qualifications of the members of the commission are the following:

- Being a civil servant.
- The chairman should be of at least equal or higher in hierarchy position as the accused person.
- At least one member of the commission should be a legal officer, a law graduate or a person who has completed training or possesses relevant experience.

Currently, there is no dedicated staff in government organisations responsible for dealing with disciplinary matters. The members of the commission of inquiry are appointed in rotation and depending on the technical expertise required for each case. Indeed, interviews with representatives of the OCSC have highlighted that public officials are reluctant in participating in commissions of inquiries for various reasons. First of all, there is the issue of personal relationships developed among colleagues in small government agencies. These types of personal relationships may endanger the independence of the investigative process. Moreover, duties related to disciplinary matters are often viewed as a "tick the box" exercise and are added on top of the daily workload of public officials. These issues directly affect the quality of the investigative process and the fairness of the disciplinary enforcement, which requires dedicated resources with adequate tools, specific skills and understanding in order to be effective and efficient.

According to information provided during fact-finding meetings, Thai government agencies suffer indeed a lack of personnel with appropriate expertise, such as a specialisation in disciplinary law and a background on disciplinary investigative techniques. This is a critical element to ensure the effectiveness of disciplinary proceedings. Ensuring training and building professionalism of enforcement officials not only limit discretional choices, but also help address technical challenges, ensure a consistent approach and reduce the rate of annulled sanctions due to procedural mistakes and poor quality of investigations (OECD, 2020[5]).

There are two options that Thailand could consider to overcome these bottlenecks, build knowledge on disciplinary matters and increase the capacity of the disciplinary enforcement system to respond to alleged integrity violations:

1. Consider establishing a registry of trained disciplinary investigators with appropriate legal and investigative background to ensure professionalisation and the quality of the disciplinary process:

   This approach would require investing efforts in a specialised training for disciplinary investigations and provide appropriate incentives for public officials with a fitting professional and academic background to participate. In that context, Thailand could strengthen the capacity of disciplinary investigators by creating specific job profiles that reflect the mandate and tasks required to carry out the investigations (OECD, 2020[5]). Incentives could include a variety of options ranging from financial remuneration to certifications. As far as the specialised training is concerned the OCSC is developing a comprehensive training on disciplinary proceedings, which is being updated with a special course (2020-21) (see Table 1.3). It includes targeted modules on how to conduct disciplinary investigations covering a wide range of topics, such as investigation rules, accusation, determining sanctions, etc. The training should be obligatory for all public officials participating in investigative processes. This approach towards a standardised training would also ensure the consistency of investigations and limit potential discretions.

   The OCSC and PACC would be best placed to lead the development and management of this registry.

Table 1.3. Overview of OCSC training on disciplinary investigations

General Course		Special Course (currently being updated)	
Subject/Topic	**Duration (Hr)**	**Subject/Topic**	**Duration (Hr)**
Purpose and guidelines for disciplinary process. Roles and Ethics of Disciplinary Actors.	3	Psychology of investigation and recording.	6
Civil Service Discipline	6	Techniques and art of investigation.	6
Investigation Rules and Procedures.	9	Writing an investigation report and preparation of Investigation Report	9
Accusation.	3	Disciplinary Seminar.	6
How to set Investigation issues/points.	3	Administrative issues Seminar.	3
Investigation techniques.	3		
Evidences Considering.	3		
Investigation Report Examination.	3		
Fault Consideration and Punishment Determination. Punishments.	3		
Principles of conducting an investigation report.	3		
Conducting investigations and reporting Investigation.	9		
The law of administrative affairs related to Civil Service Discipline.	3		
The law on Prevention and Suppression of Corruption.	3		
Important administrative cases regarding discipline and disciplinary action	3		
The law of Officials Liability for violation	3		
Protecting the moral system according to Civil Service Act B.E.2551 (2008)	3		

Source: Materials provided by OCSC.

The OCSC, as the main agency responsible for disciplinary matters in the public sector, as well as for developing guidance, standards and training could take the lead in this initiative in co-ordination with the government agencies. Currently, HR departments of government agencies collect information about potential members of the commission of inquiry and have developed a type of catalogue from which the members of the commission are selected to participate in disciplinary investigations. However, the same public officials end up carrying out the investigations because of the reluctance to participate. To that end, a centralised approach through developing job descriptions and a registry of trained investigators under the monitoring of the OCSC would be preferable.

2. Consider establishing shared disciplinary services under a centralised entity, in order to enhance the quality of disciplinary investigations and address resources limitations:

Disciplinary systems take many forms (Table 1.4). They may be the responsibility of a centralised entity or decentralised in all government entities. Many countries have mixed systems by which less serious offences are dealt with by the entity or agency to which the public official is attached, while serious offences are within a centralised body or tribunal (Bacio Terracino, 2019[6]). Thailand follows a mixed system where serious corruption offences are dealt with by the NACC and/or the PACC, while government agencies retain the mandate regarding less serious disciplinary offences. However, as mentioned above, government agencies face serious constraints in effectively enforcing integrity standards related to the close relationships developed between public officials as well as a lack of resources. To address this challenge, Thailand could consider piloting shared disciplinary offices or "outsourcing" the mandate to conduct disciplinary investigations to one of the existing central anti-corruption agencies.

Table 1.4. Comparative overview of administrative procedures in selected countries

Country	Investigations and hearings	Sanctioning decisions	Enforcing sanctions
Brazil	1) Simplified TCA procedure for minor cases (including admission of guilt).	Line ministries for TCA and inquiries.	Line ministries and the National Disciplinary Board
	2) Formal inquiry (*sindicancias*) by line ministries for less serious offences.	Line ministries for TCA and inquiries.	
	3) Temporary PAD commission of three civil servants (administrative disciplinary process, PAD) for serious offences.	For serious offences, a PAD commission can propose the application of a sanction (including dismissal) to the line ministry and the National Disciplinary Board. These enforcing authorities cannot dissent from the PAD's proposition without proper justification.	
Germany	Individual line ministries	Individual line ministries	Individual line ministries
Hong Kong	ICAC	ICAC to provide recommendations	Individual line ministries
Mexico (under recent reforms under the National Anti-corruption System, secondary implementing legislation pending)	1) Internal control bodies (SFP, Ministry of Public Administration) for minor offences.	Internal control bodies (SFP, Ministry of Public Administration) for minor offences.	Individual line ministries
	2) Administrative Fiscal Tribunal (Tribunal Federal de Justicia Administrativa) for serious cases.	Administrative Fiscal Tribunal for serious cases	
Netherlands	Individual line ministries	Individual line ministries	Individual line ministries
Singapore	CPIB	CPIB to provide recommendations	Individual line ministries

Source: Adapted from (OECD, 2017[7]).

As far as the shared model is concerned, several countries have been implementing similar approaches in the field of internal audit, to address challenges arising from reduced budgets. For example, the UK has been working on developing a shared audit services model by consolidating internal audit services, moving from the departmental structure to a single integrated audit service, the Government Internal Audit Agency (GIAA). The GIAA is responsible for providing individual departmental audit and assurance services across government and the development of the profession across government.

This model can be used in an adapted version for establishing dedicated but shared disciplinary offices in Thailand. The principle behind creating shared offices is to have sufficient numbers of disciplinary investigators grouped for the development of capabilities. Moreover, it results in various benefits deriving from the building of expertise, leading practices and improving the efficiency and quality of the overall system while reducing the financial cost (OECD, 2017[8]).

Establishing reasonable timeframes for the conclusion of each step of the investigation is needed to ensure timeliness and efficiency

Fair and effective enforcement mechanisms depend on the timely initiation and conclusion of proceedings. This applies to pre-trial investigations as well as judicial court proceedings, and is equally relevant in criminal and disciplinary systems. In case of a serious disciplinary breach, the CSC Regulation on Disciplinary Proceedings, B.E. 2556 (2013) establishes a timeframe of 120 days to complete the investigation process, starting with the first meeting of the commission of inquiry (Table 1.5). In comparison, the period for the conclusion of the disciplinary process under the PACC is two years, starting from the reception of the allegation and including the imposition of sanctions.

Table 1.5. Duration of disciplinary investigation for a serious disciplinary breach in government agencies

Process	Duration
Once the order of appointment of the commission of inquiry is acknowledged: • Directions meeting • Notification and explanation of allegations	
Taking evidence from the party making the allegation • Notice of allegation • Summary of evidence supporting the allegation	
Taking evidence from the accused public officials • Resolution • Disciplinary investigation report • Submission of dossier	
	Total: 120 days

Note: The timeframe may be extended as necessary for not more than 60 days (per extension). If the inquiry is not completed within 180 days, the person appointing the commission of inquiry must report to the Ministry CSSC.
Source: (OCSC, 2014[2]).

Without specific timeframes for each step of the investigation, the risk of increased time pressure at the end of the investigative period emerges, jeopardising the quality of the investigation as a whole. Therefore, in order to ensure the timely advancement of the investigation, Thailand may set indicative or fixed maximum timeframes for each step of the investigation process. The OCSC and PACC would be best placed to lead the process of establishing the fixed maximum timeframes for each step of the investigation process.

In general, timeliness needs to be balanced with the inherent complexity that often comes with disciplinary proceedings and usually depends on the specific circumstances of each case. Therefore, it is difficult to determine a threshold for the timely disciplinary enforcement of integrity standards and even for criminal enforcement international legal instruments have not established specific timeframes for what constitutes a "reasonable time".

Both the disciplinary process followed within government agencies and within the PACC highlight that Thailand has been able to establish effective thresholds for the timely conclusion of the investigative process. However, as far proceedings in government agencies are concerned, these timeframes do not include the imposition of sanctions by the supervising official, which is not subject to any time limitations. This can lead to excessive delays in carrying out enforcement proceedings, undermine the rule of law and ultimately prevent access to justice. Lengthy processes for the imposition of sanctions may endanger the principle of legal certainty and the validity of evidence, which may deteriorate over time, and thereby prevent the accused from exercising their fundamental rights (OECD, 2017[7]).

This is particularly the case in Thailand, where there is no statute of limitations for disciplinary misconduct and public official can be sanctioned even after leaving the government. According to Section 100 of the Civil Service Act B.E. 2551 (2008), amended in 2019, the supervising official has to impose the disciplinary sanction within 3 years as from the date that the public official left the government service. This practice may also implicate a potential waste of resources and time if proceedings are initiated, but never concluded creating a backlog of pending disciplinary cases. Indeed, if the sanction is never imposed or imposed very late this affects the whole appeal process before the MSPC and the administrative courts.

The lack of statute of limitations is not necessarily a disadvantage. In fact, several OECD member and partner countries, such as Brazil and Germany pose no formal statute of limitations, while in Mexico this is 3 or 7 years depending on the seriousness of the offence (OECD, 2017[7]). However, thresholds should be in place to ensure at least the timeliness of disciplinary investigations. An effective approach would be to align the time thresholds of the government agencies to those of the PACC covering the whole process from initiation to imposition of sanctions. In that way, both timeliness, as well as the rights of the accused can be preserved.

Promoting co-operation and exchange of information among institutions and entities

Streamlining the mandate for carrying out disciplinary investigations under the PACC would improve the co-ordination of disciplinary enforcement

In Thailand, allegations are received through different channels and a disciplinary investigation may be initiated by government agencies, the NACC and the PACC. The point of reception of each allegation and the type of the alleged offence determines the actor responsible for carrying out the investigation (see Table 1.1). Regardless of the point of reception, if the allegation concerns a serious corruption offence, the case is always referred for investigation to the NACC. Serious corruption offences are usually considered acts implicating criminal liability.

For all other allegations, the disciplinary investigation is conducted by the organisation that first received the allegation. This can be any government agency, the NACC or the PACC. Once the allegation is received, both the NACC and the PACC initiate preliminary investigation, during which investigators determine whether a serious corruption offence or a disciplinary offence has taken place. In that sense, criminal and disciplinary investigations run in parallel and do not affect each other, as a single act of a public official may be the source of both criminal and disciplinary responsibility

In case the investigation of the NACC or the PACC leads to a disciplinary offence, the case is referred to the respective government agency for further action and the imposition of sanctions. It should be noted that NACC or PACC investigation findings are binding for the government agencies.

Figure 1.1. Overview of disciplinary procedures for public officials in Thailand

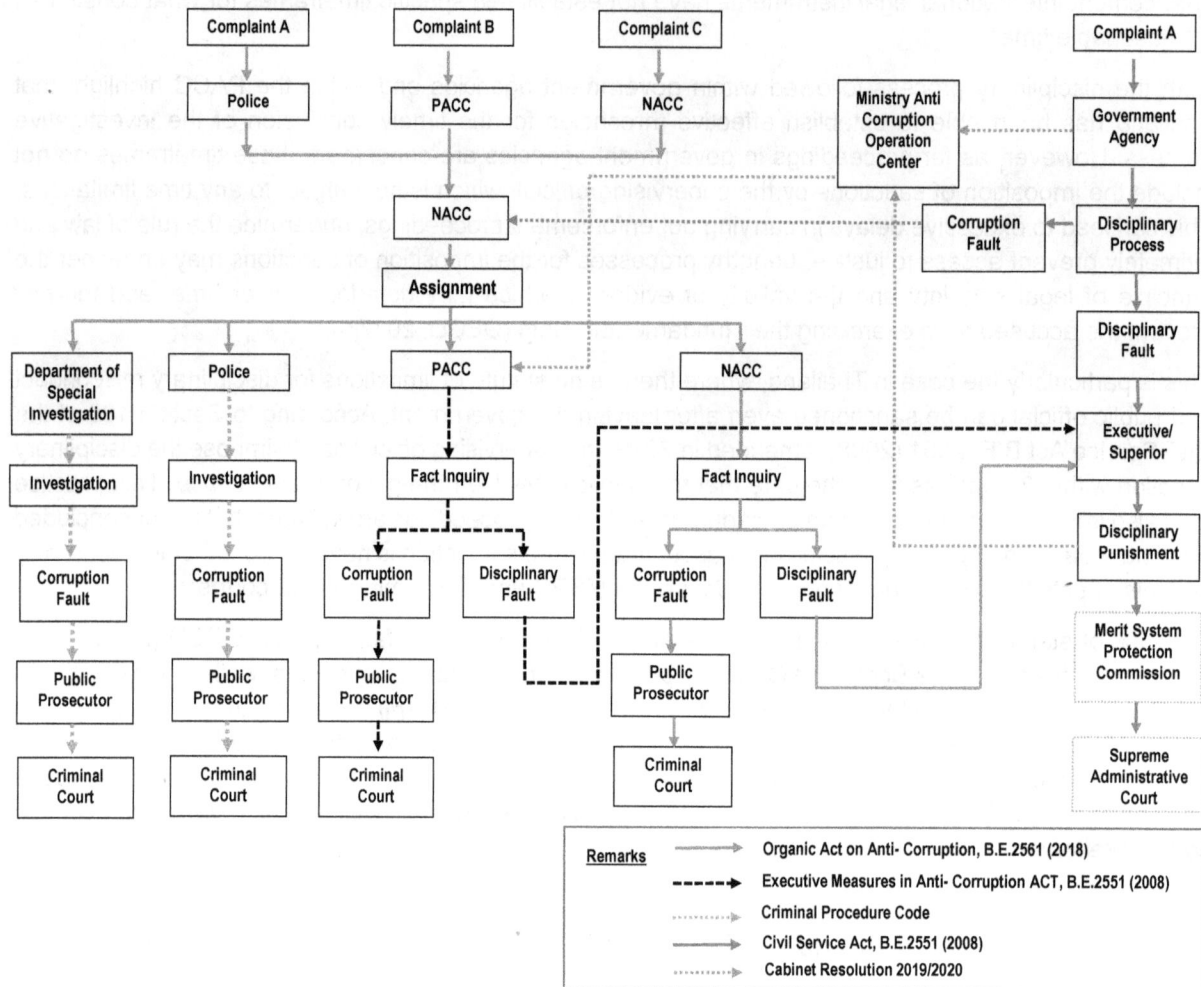

Source: Developed by Thai public officials and OECD.

To avoid potential overlaps and duplication of efforts and achieve a more co-ordinated disciplinary enforcement, each of these actors could refer complaints relevant to misconduct of public officials to the PACC for further disciplinary investigation. In that way, NACC would keep a core mandate for the criminal investigations related to corruption, while all disciplinary investigations would be streamlined through the PACC and then referred to the respective government agency for disciplinary action. PACC would be the more suitable candidate to take on the lead role in disciplinary investigations considering that it has already built sufficient expertise and a wealth of available resources that the individual government agencies lack.

Enhancing the co-operation between actors involved in the disciplinary enforcement regimes, for example by promoting regular meetings to exchange good practices

Disciplinary systems involving many different actors and investigating entities require enhanced oversight and co-ordination to achieve effectiveness. This is the case in Thailand, where an allegation about the misconduct of a public official may lead to different procedural paths depending on the agency receiving it. Although a disciplinary investigation may be conducted by one agency and the sanction imposed by another, there is no formal mechanism promoting horizontal dialogue among them.

Co-operation between stakeholders involved in the disciplinary system helps ensure uniform application of integrity standards, address common challenges, as well as promote the exchange of good practices. This can be achieved by organising regular meetings among NACC, PACC and investigators of government agencies to enable dialogue and the exchange of good practices. This initiative would provide investigators of government agencies the opportunity to engage to peer learning exercises with NACC/PACC trained investigators and address commonly faced challenges.

To improve co-ordination and exchange of information, Thailand could consider the development of an electronic case management tool

In order to achieve greater levels of maturity with regards to co-ordination mechanisms, Thailand could consider the use of electronic tools (Box 1.3), which ensure the effective management of each case. Such tools enable the control and following up on information about administrative procedures against public officials. At the same time, they provide a comprehensive mechanism to manage all the steps of cases allowing all relevant actors to follow, access or submit information for the swift advancement of disciplinary cases. Moreover, the case management tool could enable interoperability with other state digital platforms (e.g. tax/asset/interest declarations, databases of public officials involved in public procurement contracts, HR databases, etc.) with the goal of facilitating the access to information that can be used as evidence during investigations. of specific bodies that should be determined by law and without prejudice to the laws and regulations regarding data protection and confidential information.

One caveat lies in the processing of the information and data collected. To be effective, data must be accurate and proportional to the purposes for which they are collected, therefore, they should be collected and processed fairly and lawfully. In practice, this means that the agencies allowed access to such tools should be determined by law and the information collected should be used without prejudice to the laws and regulations regarding data protection and confidentiality (OECD, 2020[5]).

Box 1.3. CGU's Disciplinary Management System and the Estonian Court Information System (KIS)

One of the pillars of CGU's co-ordination function is the Disciplinary Proceedings Management System (Sistema de Gestão de Processos Disciplinares, CGU-PAD), a software allowing to store and make available, in a fast and secure way, the information about the disciplinary procedures instituted within public entities.

With the information available in the CGU-PAD, public managers can monitor and control disciplinary processes, identify critical points, construct risk maps and establish guidelines for preventing and tackling corruption and other breaches of administrative nature.

As for the Estonian Court Information System (KIS), when a court uploads a document to it, it is sent via a secure electronic layer for data exchange (the X-Road) to the e-File, a central database and case management system. The e-File allows procedural parties and their representatives to electronically submit procedural documents to courts and to observe the progress of the proceedings related to them. The document uploaded to the e-File is then visible to the relevant addressees, who are notified via email. After the addressee accesses the Public e-File and opens the uploaded document, the document is considered as legally received. KIS then receives a notification that the document has been viewed by the addressee or her/his representative. If the document is not received in the Public e-File during the concrete time-period the court uses other methods of service.

Figure 1.2. e-File and Court Information System

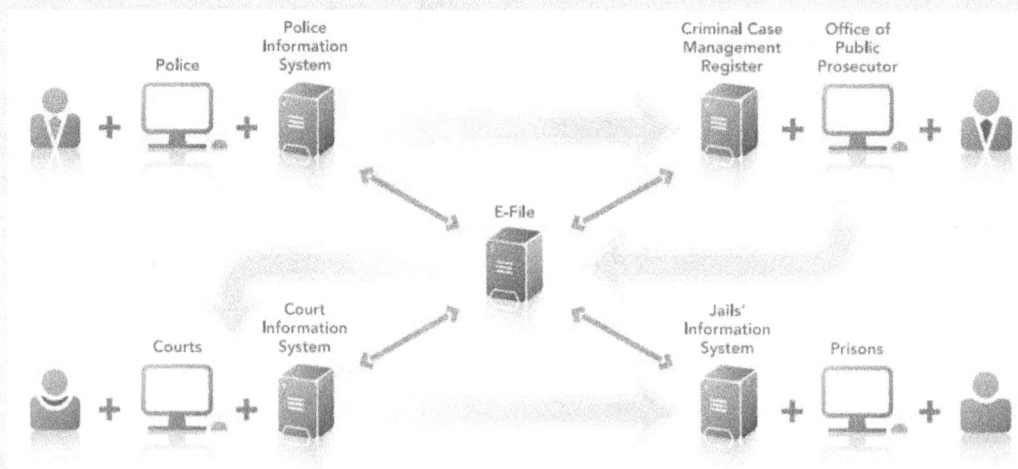

Source: CGU's website, www.gov.br/cgu/pt-br/assuntos/atividade-disciplinar; www.rik.ee/sites/www.rik.ee/files/elfinder/article_files/RIK_e_Court_Information_System%2B3mm_bleed.pdf; www.rik.ee/en/e-file.

Strengthening the co-ordinating role of the NACC to facilitate the exchange of information between the criminal and disciplinary regime and ensure a coherent approach to investigations

In Thailand, the disciplinary system works in parallel with the criminal one, as part of the wider framework for the enforcement of integrity standards. Authorities under one of those enforcement regimes may become aware of facts or information that are relevant to another regime, and they should swiftly notify them to ensure potential responsibilities are identified. Indeed, cross-agency co-ordination is particularly important during the investigative phase, where relevant information is often detected by agencies whose activity may be a source of both disciplinary and criminal responsibility. (Martini, 2014[9]). A single act by a public official may also be the source of both criminal and disciplinary responsibility, so all relevant institutions should count on each other's collaboration in order to bring them forward following respective procedures.

The parallel procedures and the different procedural safeguards applying to each regime affect the investigations. Criminal investigations demand a higher level of guarantees regarding the suspect's rights, due to the intrusive nature of the investigative powers attributed to law enforcement authorities. Administrative investigations, on the other hand, involve a much lower level of interference with the rights of individuals and do not require the same safeguards (Cardona, 2003[4]). While criminal and disciplinary enforcement systems have different objectives and functions, mechanisms should be in place to promote co-operation and exchange of information, which could be relevant to initiate or support each other's proceedings. This could take different forms, such as formalised notification mechanisms and rules to co-ordinate respective proceedings.

According to the information provided during the fact-finding interviews, the NACC already has some co-ordinating functions for initiating enforcement proceedings given that it is the only agency with the main mandate on criminal investigations. Under this role, it issues letters or requests to consult the relevant agencies. Despite the absence of any inter-agency co-ordination mechanism, Thai stakeholders have reported that the disciplinary and criminal regime run concurrently and do not affect each other. However, in many cases, the pending criminal investigations can delay the disciplinary process. To speed up procedures and ensure coherence of investigations across enforcement regimes, it is recommendable that Thailand develops co-ordination mechanisms to prevent the potential fragmentation of efforts and promote mutual learning and understanding (see Box 1.4). The NACC could naturally take the key co-ordinating role in bringing together all anti-corruption stakeholders(i.e. the Prosecutor General, the OCSC, the Ombudsman, the Anti-Corruption Centres, the State Audit Office and the internal audit departments of line ministries) to strengthen enforcement collaboration and establish channels for timely and continuous communication between them.

Box 1.4. Mechanisms to prevent fragmentation of efforts among enforcement regimes

Inter-agency agreements, memorandums of understanding, joint instructions or networks of co-operation and interaction are common mechanisms to promote co-operation with and between law enforcement authorities. Examples of this include various forms of agreements between: the prosecutors or the national anti-corruption authority and different ministries; the financial intelligence unit and other stakeholders working to combat money-laundering; or between the different law enforcement agencies themselves. These typologies of agreements are aimed at sharing intelligence on the fight against crime and corruption or carrying out other forms of collaboration.

In some cases, countries have launched formal inter-agency implementation committees or information-exchange systems (sometimes called "anti-corruption forums" or "integrity forums") among various agencies; others hold regular co-ordination meetings.

In order to foster co-operation and inter-agency co-ordination, some countries have initiated staff secondment programs among different entities in the executive and law enforcement with an anti-corruption mandate, including the national financial intelligence unit. Similarly, some other countries placed inspection personnel of the anti-corruption authority in each ministry and at the regional level.

Source: (UNODC, 2017[10]), State of Implementation of the United Nations Convention against Corruption Criminalization, Law Enforcement and International Cooperation.

Encouraging transparency about the effectiveness of the disciplinary system and the outcomes of cases

Strengthening the monitoring role of the OCSC on disciplinary enforcement and developing a framework to measure the efficiency, fairness and quality of the disciplinary system

The collection and communication of data on enforcement can support the integrity system in many ways. Firstly, statistical data about the disciplinary sanctions imposed following the integrity violation provide insights into key risk areas, which can inform the development or update of specific policies as well as integrity and anticorruption strategies. Secondly, data can feed indicators used for monitoring and evaluating integrity policies and strategies, and can help assess the performance of the disciplinary system as a whole. Thirdly, data can inform institutional communications, giving account of enforcement action to other public officials and the public (OECD, 2018[11]). Lastly, consolidated, accessible and scientific analysis of statistical data on enforcement practices enable the assessment of the effectiveness of existing measures and the operational co-ordination among anti-corruption institutions (UNODC, 2017[10]).

In Thailand, there is no standardised process regarding the collection of enforcement data. The OCSC collects several data from government agencies on imposed disciplinary sanctions (See Figure 1.3 and Figure 1 4). The data is further classified by gender and position of sanctioned public officials, as well as by offence. However, the data is not shared with the public. Upon request, the OCSC may compile information about disciplinary action taken and prepare it in writing for government agencies and interested parties. This practice is not applied by all government agencies. In comparison, the NACC may collect some data about disciplinary proceedings, which however are not publicly accessible due to confidentiality and national security reasons. In some cases, this information can be shared exceptionally upon individual request and only for the interests of the government service.

Figure 1.3. Total disciplinary sanctions issued by government agencies in fiscal years 2015-19

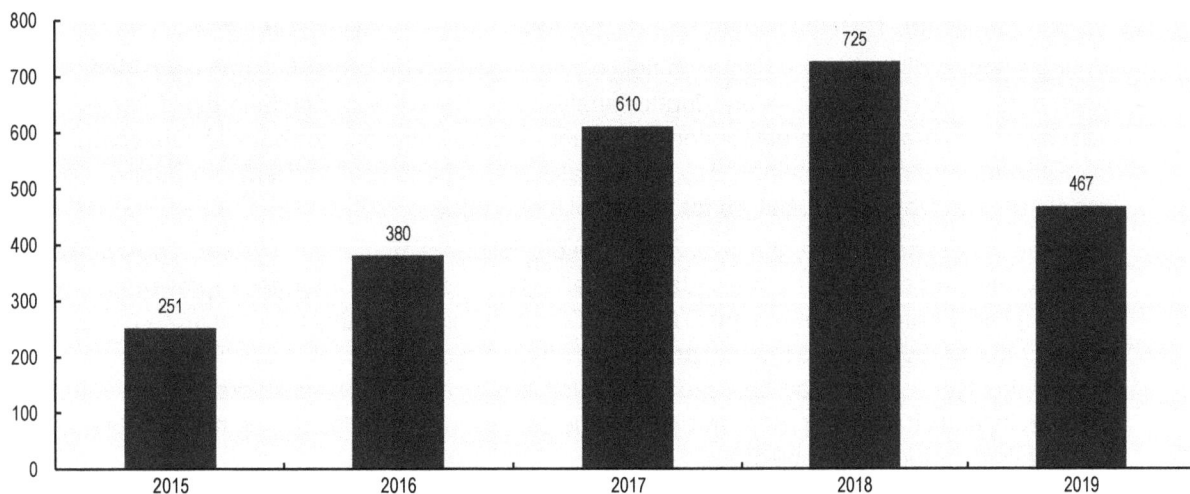

Source: Elaborated by OECD based on data provided by OCSC.

Figure 1 4. Types of sanctions, written paroles and warnings issued by government agencies in fiscal year 2019

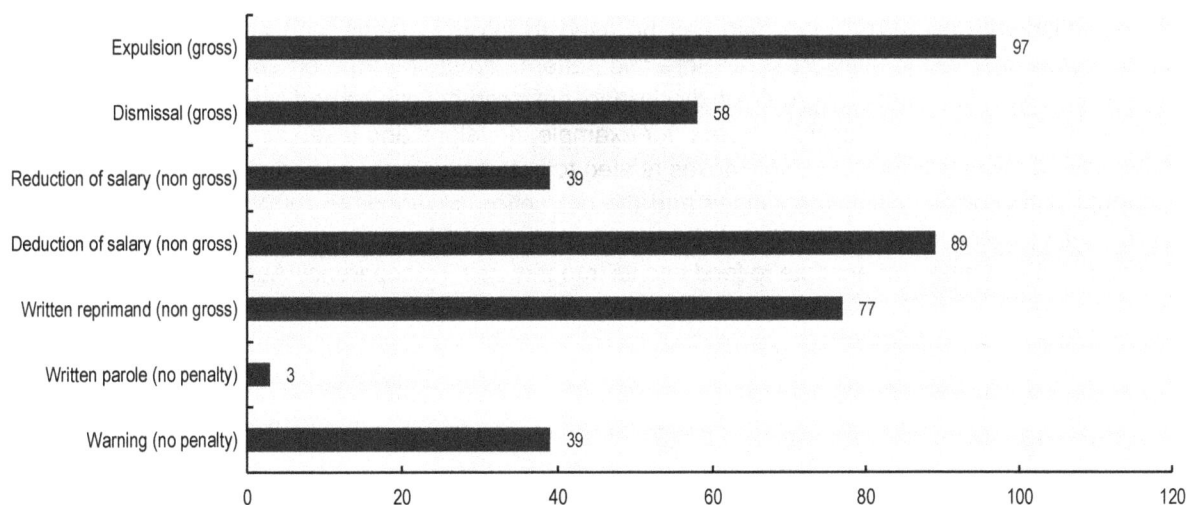

Note: "No penalty" means that in the case of a minor disciplinary breach and existence of a cause for refraining from punishment, punishment may have refrained and a written parole or warning may be issued instead (Section 96 of the Civil Service Act). These are not sanctions.
Source: Elaborated by OECD based on data provided by OCSC.

Thailand could consider explicitly assigning to the OCSC the responsibility for collecting and processing statistical data in order to monitor the efficiency and effectiveness of the disciplinary system. This would be in line with the recommended strengthened co-ordinating role of the OCSC (see further analysis in "Promoting co-operation and exchange of information among institutions and entities" section). Given its access to information through its representatives at government agencies and its natural role to design, implement and follow up on disciplinary standards, the OCSC would be well placed to take on this responsibility.

The variety of information collected by the OCSC is already a commendable feature. The next step would be to leverage this exercise to collect data systematically, and to ensure transparency and accountability of the enforcement system. This can be achieved in two ways:

1. Making selected disciplinary information publicly accessible in an interactive and user-friendly way (open data) enabling its re-use and further analysis. In this context, Thailand could consider the practice of Colombia, which elaborated corruption-related sanctions indicators, (Observatorio de Transparencia y Anticorrupción, n.d.[12]) and Brasil, which periodically collect and publish data on disciplinary sanctions in pdf and xls format. (CGU, n.d.[13]).

2. Using the data to assess the effectiveness of the disciplinary enforcement system. Through further analysis, the data collected can help identify challenges and areas for further improvements within the disciplinary enforcement regime. The OCSC can make use of this information to enhance its monitoring and oversight activities and the overall effectiveness of disciplinary proceedings. Indeed, this type of data can be used to develop key performance indicators (KPIs) identifying bottlenecks and challenging areas throughout the procedures, but also setting measurable targets for achieving performance objectives.

   Building on its current data collection practices, the OCSC could additionally collect data to design a comprehensive system for measuring the effectiveness, efficiency, quality and fairness of disciplinary proceedings. Several international organisations have developed relevant indicators (e.g. share of reported alleged offences taken forward, and average length of proceedings) for the justice system, which can be adapted to the needs and process of the disciplinary system (Council of Europe, 2018[14]).

In co-operation with the PACC, the data can be used to inform integrity and anti-corruption policies. Moreover, they can help identify areas, sectors and patterns emerging from on-going investigations and sanctions imposed. More generally, data on disciplinary enforcement can be part of the broader monitoring and evaluation of the integrity system. Korea, for example, develops and takes into consideration for the monitoring and evaluation process two indexes related to both disciplinary and criminal corruption cases - the corrupt public official disciplinary index and the corruption case index – within the annual integrity assessment of public organisations. (Anti-Corruption and Civil Rights Commission, n.d.[15]). Similarly, Thailand could use enforcement data to feed into its Integrity and Transparency Assessment (ITA).

Proposals for action

The analysis of the role and effectiveness of the disciplinary system in Thailand has shown that the country has a solid foundation in place for enforcing integrity rules and standards. However, further reforms are required to improve its quality and introduce a more coherent approach to disciplinary processes. The proposed reforms can be summarised as follows:

Ensuring fairness, objectivity and timeliness

- Consider creating additional safeguards to ensure the integrity of supervising officials and the fair imposition of sanctions.
- Consider establishing a registry of trained disciplinary investigators with appropriate legal and investigative background to ensure professionalisation and the quality of the disciplinary process.
- Consider establishing "shared" disciplinary offices under a centralised agency, in order to enhance the quality of disciplinary investigations and address resource limitations.
- Consider establishing reasonable timeframes for the conclusion of each step of the investigation is needed to ensure timeliness and efficiency.
- Consider aligning the time thresholds of the government agencies to those of the PACC covering the whole process from initiation to imposition of sanctions.

Promoting co-operation and exchange of information among institutions and entities

- Consider streamlining the mandate for carrying out disciplinary investigations under the PACC to avoid potential overlaps and duplication of efforts and achieve a more co-ordinated disciplinary enforcement.
- Consider enhancing the co-operation between actors involved in the disciplinary enforcement regimes, for example by promoting regular meetings to exchange good practices.
- Consider strengthening the co-ordinating role of the NACC to facilitate the exchange of information between the criminal and disciplinary regime and ensure a coherent approach to investigations.

Encouraging transparency about the effectiveness of the disciplinary system and the outcomes of cases

- Consider assigning the responsibility for collecting and processing statistical data to the OCSC in order to monitor the efficiency and effectiveness of the disciplinary system.
- Consider making selected disciplinary information publicly accessible in an interactive and user-friendly way (open data) enabling its re-use and further analysis;
- Consider using collected data to assess the effectiveness of the disciplinary enforcement system;
- Consider using enforcement data to inform integrity and anti-corruption policies as part of the broader monitoring and evaluation of the integrity system.

References

Anti-Corruption and Civil Rights Commission (n.d.), *Assessing Integrity of Public Organizations*, http://www.acrc.go.kr/en/board.do?command=searchDetail&method=searchList&menuId=020 3160302. [15]

Bacio Terracino, J. (2019), "Article 8: Code of Conduct for Public Officials", in Rose, C., M. Kubiciel and O. Landwehr (eds.), *The United Nations Convention Against Corruption: A Commentary*, Oxford University Press, Oxford. [6]

Cardona, F. (2003), *Liabilities and discipline of civil servants*, OECD, Paris, http://www.sigmaweb.org/publicationsdocuments/37890790.pdf. [4]

CGU (n.d.), *Relatórios de Punições Expulsivas*, http://www.cgu.gov.br/assuntos/atividade-disciplinar/relatorios-de-punicoes-expulsivas (accessed on 30 July 2019). [13]

Council of Europe (2018), *European judicial systems. Efficiency and quality of justice. Edition 2018 (2016 data)*, https://rm.coe.int/rapport-avec-couv-18-09-2018-en/16808def9c (accessed on 30 July 2019). [14]

Martini (2014), "Investigating Corruption: Good Practices in Specialised Law Enforcement", *Anti-corruption Helpdesk*, Transparency International, https://knowledgehub.transparency.org/assets/uploads/helpdesk/Investigating_corruption_go od_practice_in_specialised_law_enforcement_2014.pdf. [9]

Observatorio de Transparencia y Anticorrupción (n.d.), *Indicador de Sanciones Disciplinarias*, http://www.anticorrupcion.gov.co/Paginas/indicador-sanciones-disciplinarias.aspx (accessed on 30 July 2019). [12]

OCSC (2014), *Disciplinary Proceedings pursuant to the Civil Service Act B.E. 2551 (2008)*, Bureau of Disciplinary Standards, Office of the Civil Service Commission, Thailand. [2]

OECD (2020), *OECD Public Integrity Handbook*, OECD Publishing, Paris, https://dx.doi.org/10.1787/ac8ed8e8-en. [5]

OECD (2018), *Integrity for Good Governance in Latin America and the Caribbean: From Commitments to Action*, OECD Publishing, Paris, https://dx.doi.org/10.1787/9789264201866-en. [11]

OECD (2017), "Enforcing integrity: Strengthening Mexico's administrative disciplinary regime for public officials", in *OECD Integrity Review of Mexico: Taking a Stronger Stance Against Corruption*, OECD Publishing, Paris, https://dx.doi.org/10.1787/9789264273207-9-en. [3]

OECD (2017), *OECD Integrity Review of Colombia: Investing in Integrity for Peace and Prosperity*, OECD Public Governance Reviews, OECD Publishing, Paris, https://dx.doi.org/10.1787/9789264278325-en. [8]

OECD (2017), *OECD Integrity Review of Peru: Enhancing Public Sector Integrity for Inclusive Growth*, OECD Public Governance Reviews, OECD Publishing, Paris, https://dx.doi.org/10.1787/9789264271029-en. [7]

OECD (2017), *OECD Recommendation of the Council on Public Integrity*, OECD, Paris, http://www.oecd.org/gov/ethics/OECD-Recommendation-Public-Integrity.pdf. [1]

UNODC (2017), *State of Implementation of the United Nations Convention against Corruption Criminalization, Law Enforcement and International Cooperation*, http://www.unodc.org/unodc/en/corruption/tools_and_publications/state_of_uncac_implementation.html. [10]

Notes

[1] National Police Act B.E. 2547 (2004).

[2] Act on Judicial Service of the Courts of Justice B.E. 2543 (2000).

[3] Local Personnel Administration Act B.E. 2542 (1999).

[4] A supervising official is usually a director general or above. The Civil Service Act defines the supervising official as the person authorised to make an instatement order under Section 57 of the Act (OCSC, 2014[2]).

2 Integrity risk management in Thailand: Immediate challenges and areas for improvement

This chapter describes the national government's efforts in Thailand to modernise risk management policies and practices for safeguarding integrity. This includes the work of the Comptroller General's Department (CGD), the Office of the National Anti-Corruption Commission (NACC) and the Office of the Office of the Public Sector Anti-Corruption Commission (PACC), which play critical roles in supporting line ministries to build their knowledge, capacity and skills for managing integrity risks. The chapter offers recommendations for the Thai government to consider in three areas: 1) ensuring clarity of roles and making good governance a central theme; 2) improving risk assessments; and 3) enhancing monitoring and evaluation, as well as quality assurance assessments. These areas are not exhaustive with regards to the challenges and opportunities for improving control and oversight in Thailand more broadly, but they represent key priorities given the narrow scope of the chapter on integrity risk management.

Introduction

In the past three years, Thailand has made legal and regulatory reforms that sought to modernise the internal control system in line with international standards, such as those established by the Committee of the Sponsoring Organisation of the Treadway Commission (COSO) and the Institute of Internal Auditors (IIA). By improving the legal and policy frameworks for internal control, risk management and internal audit functions, Thai policy makers have signalled the need to balance an enforcement-focused model with preventive approaches.

While recent reforms have aided in modernisation, the Thai government faces a number of challenges to implement reforms. The responsibility for facing these challenges is shared across the Thai government. One of the key institutions is the Comptroller General's Department (CGD), which is the centralised internal audit function in the Thai government. As part of the reform process, the CGD took over key responsibilities for internal control from the State Audit Office (SAO). Other central bodies that are critical allies for the CGD in advancing internal control and risk management in government are the Office of the National Anti-Corruption Commission (NACC) and the Office of the Public Sector Anti-Corruption Commission (PACC). In addition, managers in government have many of the core responsibilities to implement recent changes to strengthen internal control and risk management for safeguarding integrity. For this reason, it is critical that these individuals on the frontlines understand the value of and benefits from internal control and risk management first hand.

This chapter elaborates on key challenges and recommends actions for the Thai government, particularly the CGD and managers in agencies, to further improve integrity risk management and assessments. The chapter focuses on the following overarching issues:

- **Ensuring clarity of roles and making good governance a central theme:** While reforms are still fresh, risk assessments can be positioned as management tools for better governance as opposed to compliance exercises. Doing so requires improvements to standards and guidelines to ensure clarity of roles and responsibilities for managing risks and further demonstrating the value of risk management for everyday operations and control decisions. The CGD and other government-wide entities can help to advance this governance-oriented mindset, in particular, by demonstrating the value of risk management, control and audit for achieving policy goals, as well as means to demonstrate the government's transparency and accountability to citizens.

- **Overcoming implementation challenges to better manage and assess risks:** Thailand's recent legal reforms have further codified the need for risk-based approaches, and there are existing tools to build on, including the Integrity and Transparency Assessment. However, the government faces new challenges for assessing integrity risks, particularly across levels of government, as it modernises its risk management policies and practices. The need for harmonising existing approaches and offering more guidance is a key issue facing the CGD, in addition to addressing gaps in capacity and knowledge for conducting risk assessments at national and regional levels.

- **Enhancing monitoring and evaluation, as well as quality assurance assessments:** With several parallel efforts in Thailand to safeguard integrity and manage risks, effective monitoring and evaluation (M&E) is critical for ensuring an effective internal control system and the fulfilment of policy goals and objectives. The CGD developed a process for quality assurance assessments, which is a positive signal and recognition of the need for monitoring and evaluation (M&E) and continuous improvement of internal audit activities. The CGD can take additional steps to develop M&E plans concerning integrity risk management in particular, in line with the OECD's Recommendation on Public Integrity.[1]

These areas represent critical, but not *all,* areas for improvement to advance integrity risk management in Thailand. Responses of Thai officials to OECD questionnaires and input during interviews focused largely on legal and policy concerns, given recent reforms. Therefore, recommendations and findings related to integrity risk management in practice are limited, including key issues such as managing and assessing risks at the provincial level and methodological considerations for risk assessments. Some of these issues may be be addressed in subsequent phases of co-operation.

Ensuring clarity of roles and making good governance a central theme

Enhance the focus on integrity in standards and rules, and clarify roles and responsibilities within the internal control system

After the passage of new laws and standards in recent years, Thailand has developed a strong foundation for internal control, risk management and internal audit in the public sector. The State Fiscal and Financial Disciplines Act, B.E. 2561 (2018) applies to all public entities, including state-owned enterprises, and it stipulates that government entities should establish an internal control system in compliance with standards and rules prescribed by the Ministry of Finance (Section 79). The Act also defines managerial control and civil servants' responsibilities related to internal control and risk management. To complement this Act, the CGD within the Ministry of Finance recently developed the *Risk Management Standards and Practical Rules for State Agencies, B.E. 2562 (2019)*. It focuses on13 practical rules for risk management, which includes a general reference to the need of public institutions to conduct risk assessments.

The CGD is also responsible for setting internal audit standards, including the *2017 Internal Audit Standards and Ethics for Internal Auditing of Government Agencies*, which draws from the Institute of Internal Auditors' (IIA) International Standards for the Professional Practice of Internal Auditing. Other actors in government have developed additional materials related specifically to managing corruption risks. This includes central bodies like the NACC and the PACC, as well as individual line ministries, which produce their own frameworks and guidelines for managing integrity and corruption risks in the government's daily operations.

The legal and policy foundation for the internal control system in Thailand, including managerial control, risk management and internal audit is extensive, but can also create confusion in the context of integrity and anti-corruption measures. First, corruption and fraud risks are explicitly addressed in internal audit standards, including the role of internal audit to assess such risks, but they are not directly addressed in the Rules. This sends a message that the management of fraud and corruption risks is the responsibility of the internal audit function. The CGD could amend the Rules to include a specific reference to integrity risks to avoid artificially separating this type of risk from the broader policies, practices and tools used to assess risk management in general. This would also reinforce the notion that corruption risk management is also the responsibility of managers within line ministries.

In addition, the CGD could amend standards or provide additional guidance to further clarify the role of the internal audit function for integrity risk management vis-à-vis managers. For instance, the Ministry of Finance's internal audit standards note, "Internal audit operations must assess the likelihood of corruption, and methods of managing risks related to fraud" (Ministry of Finance, 2018[1]). They also include requirements for internal audit to report fraud to heads of government and the audit committee, if applicable. Yet, the *Risk Management Standards and Practical Rules for State Agencies* say the internal audit function should not be responsible for risk management. The Rules stipulate that the head of each government agency is responsible for appointing a lead for risk management, which can be an individual or a team. Interviews with Thai officials and responses to questionnaires confirmed that internal audit functions in government agencies are leading risk management activities in practice, including carrying out risk assessments.

The CGD can address this confusion and ensure consistency of its standards and guidance so that government officials know their roles and responsibilities within the internal control system. In particular, the internal audit function should not have the primary responsibility for managing and assessing integrity risks. The IIA's Three Lines Model can be instructive for how the Thai government can define roles and responsibilities.[2] This could include revising the 2017 *Internal Audit Standards and Ethics for Internal Auditing of Government Agencies* to make it clear that internal auditors should not be leading risk assessments. Integrity risk management is primarily the responsibility of managers (i.e. the first line), as Thailand's own Practice Rules for Risk Management outlines. In addition, the CGD could consider improving self-assessment tools to further promote responsibility, accountability and the authority of managers with regards to internal control and risk management. For instance, the OECD SIGMA programme has developed guidelines for assessing the quality of internal control systems (Boryczka, Bochnar and Larin, 2019[2]). See Box 2.1 for an example of such a tool from the Netherlands (The Dutch Ministry of Finance, March 2018[3]).

Box 2.1. Netherland's Ministry of Finance self-assessment tool

The National Academy for Finance and Economy (NAFE) of the Dutch Ministry of Finance developed a self-assessment tool to improve public governance, focusing on financial management control (FMC) as a key component of public internal control. The NAFE developed an FMC assessment matrix as a practical tool to support assessments of FMC policies and practices at an institutional level, as well as to aid follow-up evaluations and actions to strengthen FMC. According to the NAFE, reasons for developing such tools include:

- FMC lacks behind the development of internal audit.
- Key elements of FMC are in place, such as financial departments and reporting systems, but operational and implementation challenges remain (including those subsequently listed).
- Excessive operational control by top management.
- Second Line of Defence, i.e., risk management, oversight and monitoring are undeveloped.
- Financial divisions do not support planning and control, except for control of the budget.
- Lack of an entity-wide planning and control mechanism, as well as planning and control at the operational level.
- Blurred lines of responsibility between the second and third lines of defence, i.e., between risk management and the internal audit function.
- Lack of key performance indicators.

The NAFE's FMC assessment matrix allows management to understand the design of their organisation assessed against good practice criteria, drawing from the European Union's principles of Public Internal Financial Control (PIFC). Assessors must have excellent knowledge of PIFC, including managerial accountability elements. In addition to managers using the matrix as a self-assessment for their department, internal auditors can make use of the matrix during an entity-wide assessment of currently running FMC systems. Effective implementation of the self-assessment methodology, including completion of the FMC matrix, results in insights about possible actions to improve the FMC configuration and practices. The matrix and results can be shared with management and staff. The table below shows the header row of the matrix followed by an example of how each column can be populated. An actual matrix would include all key components of the internal control system, such as the internal audit function, as well as many other key variables and assessment impacts.

Table 2.1. Illustrative example of select components of an FMC assessment matrix

Key component of internal control	Key variables	Assessment aspects	Indicators	Sources	Methodological approach
FMC within the primary processes/ programmes /projects (I)	Configuration of Managerial Accountability (composition of the accountability triangle: Responsibility, Accountability and Authority) (I.1)	Responsibility: there is a delegated mandate structure (tasks/obligations) described which is aligned with the organisational structure	FMC within the primary processes/programmes /projects (I)	Configuration of Managerial Accountability (composition of the accountability triangle: Responsibility, Accountability and Authority) (I.1)	Responsibility: there is a delegated mandate structure (tasks/obligations) described which is aligned with the organisational structure.
	Alignment of the managerial accountability configuration (I.2)	Responsibilities are well aligned and in balance with accountability obligations and granted authorities (I.2.1)	Alignment of the three elements of the accountability triangle	Internal regulations/process /programme descriptions	Study relevant internal regulations and assess to what extent the responsibilities, accountability and authorities are balanced with each other
FMC through supportive oversight/ controlling /monitoring processes (II)	Managerial Accountability (II.1)	Responsibility: The division of tasks and responsibilities between supportive second-line functions and first-line departments is clear and unambiguous. (II.1.1)	It is clear how division of tasks and responsibilities between first-line primary processes and second-line supportive functions are divided	Internal regulations/ procedures Operational Management Management of supportive functions (e.g. financial department, planning department, HR, IT)	Check the internal regulations/procedures and see if a clear division of tasks between first and second line can be distinguished. Is it described at all? In interviews: try to determine if the division of tasks matches the philosophy of first and second line or not. If the distinction between first and second line is blurry: describe it

Source: (The Dutch Ministry of Finance, March 2018[3]).

Finally, the FMC assessment matrix relies on the Institute of Internal Auditors' Three Lines Model. In particular, according to this model, operational managers are the first line. They are responsible for implementing and maintaining effective internal control while assessing risks to operations and strategic objectives. The various oversight, risk management and compliance functions overseeing the operational management make up the second line. These functions are responsible for support, monitoring, oversight and control over the first line. The internal audit function is the third line, and it provides independent assurance on the functioning of the first two lines. Each of these three "lines" are reflected in the FMC assessment matrix, since they play distinct roles within the organisation's wider governance framework.

Source: The Dutch Ministry of Finance (March 2018[3]), *Good Financial Governance and Public Internal Control, Presentation to the OECD.*

Unclear roles and responsibilities can undermine the independence of internal audit functions and lead to a compliance-oriented approach to risk management and internal control. Many agencies in Thailand's government do not have experience in risk management, according to Thai officials. Addressing these issues at the early stages of Thailand's efforts will help to avoid the institutionalisation of systemic and long-term challenges, and ensure that resources and training on managing and assessing risks are targeted at the right people.

Refine communication strategies to demonstrate the added value of risk management for safeguarding integrity and improving governance

The CGD, along with the NACC, the PACC and leadership of line ministries, can enhance future guidance and communications about risk management and control by having coherent messages that promote managerial ownership and risk management as a tool for better governance. In interviews with Thai officials, line ministries tend to view the risk management plan required by the CGD's *Risk Management Standards and Practical Rules for State Agencies* as a compliance exercise. This *2017 Internal Audit Standards and Ethics for Internal Auditing of Government Agencies*, which assigns corruption and fraud risk assessments to the internal audit function, only reinforces this perception.

Following recent reforms in Thailand, the integration of risk management into the operations of line ministries depends on how well managers understand and see evidence of the value of risk management for governance and the achievement of objectives. If managers do not see the value of risk management for making decisions and solving problems, they will have little commitment to integrate risk-based thinking into operations and therefore a risk-informed culture is unlikely to take root. The CGD, the NACC and the PACC can enhance guidance with positive messages that emphasise a perspective on risk management and control that is oriented towards good governance and achieving the results of policies and goals, rather than compliance with laws and standards. Similarly, they can communicate perspectives on risk assessments oriented towards solutions management, as opposed to check-the-box exercises.

In addition, messages about the value of risk management or assessments should avoid causal linkages to improvements in Transparency International's Corruption Perception Index (CPI). For instance, in responses to the OECD's questionnaire, respondents of the National Economic and Social Development Council (NESDC) indicated that most public sector entities realise the importance of risk management as a proactive measure to prevent corruption in Thailand, as well as "an essential tool for enhancing Thailand's Corruption Perception Index". Respondents added that the aim is for Thailand to rise in the CPI to become one of the "top twenty" in the world by the year 2030, in line with the *Master Plan Under the National Strategy* initiated by Prime Minister Prayuth Chan-Ocha's government (Government of Thailand, 2017[4]). The Fraud Risk Management Plan for fiscal year 2019 of the (NESDC) makes a similar assertion. It directly links risk management to changes in the CPI by stating, "fraud risk assessment is a risk management tool that helps to raise the [CPI] score" (National Economic and Social Development Council of Thailand, 2019[5]).

The examples above signal a fundamental misunderstanding about risk management, risk assessments and their purposes, as well as the CPI. The CPI cannot be used to measure the performance of specific actions taken to address corruption or to mitigate risks, and raising the score should not be a policy objective. There is no causal linkage between day-to-day risk management and the CPI, since many factors contribute to the CPI and isolating the effect of risk management on public perception is unrealistic. In many countries, the CPI is used as an input for risk assessments that provide broad context about the environment. However, by linking integrity risk management to changes in the CPI, it creates the impression that the CPI can be a performance metric for the quality and effectiveness of integrity risk management and assessments at an institutional level. This also risks undermining the concept of risk management as a critical tool for managers to support decision making and drive results related to objectives. In the 2018 Integrity Review of Thailand, the OECD highlighted the limitations of using the CPI as a diagnostic tool and recommended different types of indicators for the government to evaluate anti-corruption policies. Box 2.2 provides additional insights on the CPI, its benefits and its limitations as a diagnostic tool.

Box 2.2. Transparency International's corruption perception index: Uses and limitations as a diagnostic tool

The CPI score is a composite index combining at least three data sources per country. The confidence intervals are relatively large, and as a result, it is not possible to make scientifically reliable comparisons between countries with similar scores. Such large confidence intervals and the variability of measurements in other countries cast doubt on the reliability of the rankings: if a country falls a few places in the ranking, it may not, in fact, reflect a real deterioration in the conditions on the ground. Moreover, the CPI score is a national score, and does not reflect regional or sectoral trends and developments. The CPI is thus not suitable as a diagnostic tool. It is a perception index, and it is unclear whether fluctuating perception scores reflect real changes in levels of corruption, or simply general discontent or a response to media exposure of scandals. The CPI is not an appropriate tool for evaluating anti-corruption and integrity policies.

A balanced set of policy indicators could instead be considered, as a framework to replace the CPI as a policy target and as a measure of the progress of the anti-corruption policy. This new set of measurements could assess policy effectiveness, identify areas or institutions at risk, and inform policy planning. Specific indicators can be used to measure budget transparency, integrity in public procurement, efficiency of administrative processes, open government, as well as benchmarks related to organisational integrity, asset declaration systems and whistle-blower protection. Moreover, sector-specific indicators can be used to measure integrity in service delivery in health, education or in areas such as licencing or business creation. It may be assumed that these indicators will help improve the CPI score in the long run.

Source: OECD (2018[6]), *OECD Integrity Review of Thailand: Towards Coherent and Effective Integrity Policies.*

The CGD, NACC and PACC, as entities with government-wide responsibilities, can play a critical role in changing, or at a minimum, diversifying this message and promoting the added-value added of risk management. As discussed, this can include positive, governance-focused statements about the contributions of the results of risk management and assessments to an effective control environment. This could include messages about risk management supporting managers in making informed decisions to find solutions to mitigate risks related to organisational objectives, as opposed to raising the score in the CPI or addressing broad sets of environmental risks that are outside the purview of an individual line ministry.

Overcoming implementation challenges to better manage and assess integrity risks

Improve risk management guidance, including clarifying the purpose of different types of risk assessments

The Risk *Management Standards and Practical Rules for State Agencies* lay the foundation for a risk-based approach to governance and control in Thailand's government. Additional guidance could help to educate agencies as to how to implement them to ensure consistency and harmonisation. Line ministries have wide discretion in how they apply the Rules, and there are at least three different risk assessments that agencies conduct, including the following:

1. Managers are responsible for a risk assessment at the entity level, which according to the new Rules, every government agency must conduct on an annual basis as part of their risk

management plans. This type of risk assessment is in its second year of implementation. Laws and regulations do not require line ministries to submit the risk management plan or the results of the risk assessments to the Ministry of Finance. The format for documenting the risk analysis is left to the discretion of line ministries. Corruption and fraud risks are not taken into account as part of these risk assessments, as discussed.

2. The internal audit function carries out the second type of risk assessment. As noted, this role for the internal audit function is outlined in *Ministry* of *Finance's* regulations on *standards* and *guidelines* of *internal audit* for *government* agencies B.E. 2561 (2018), which state that the internal audit must assess and address fraud risks. (Ministry of Finance, 2018[1]).

3. The third type of evaluation is the Integrity and Transparency Assessment (ITA). The ITA is an evaluation that focuses on fraud and corruption in line ministries, as described in greater detail in the next section. Thai agencies have been conducting these evaluations since 2014. In the 2018 *Integrity Review of Thailand*, the OECD offered recommendations to improve the methodology, knowledge sharing and co-ordination of the ITA. To what extent the ITA or risk assessments fulfil the CGD's requirements related to risk management in practice, as defined in the Rules, is unclear.

   The ITA is a core element of component Strategy 4, "Development of proactive corruption prevention systems system to counter corruption" of the National Anti-Corruption Strategy, Phase 3 (2017-2021)". The ITA is an annual assessment at the organisational level across government institutions at national and regional levels. The assessment methodology was adapted from the Anti-Corruption and Civil Rights Commission of South Korea, and was then developed and integrated to match with the transparency indicator of the NACC. The NACC, along with the PACC, lead the implementation. The methodology consists of three surveys, which cover 10 topics, including corruption prevention.[3]

PACC officials communicated the development of a fourth approach, called a "Risk Assessment System," for detecting corruption and misconduct in the public sector. The system envisions three levels—policy, ministerial/departmental and provincial. The system at the policy level entails developing polices and consistent criteria for fraud risk indicators, guided by the work of the NACC. At the ministerial or departmental level, the system involves designating ACOCs as the leads for carrying out fraud risk assessments related to service delivery, the use of authority, and budget spending and management of resources. Lastly, ACOCs would also conduct assessments at the provincial level, focusing on programmes with large budgets. At the time of drafting this report, the Risk Assessment System is in the conceptual stage and could not be assessed for effectiveness or harmonisation with existing efforts in terms of its design or implementation. The recommendations below take into account these four parallel efforts.

The CGD, in co-ordination with the NACC and the PACC, can offer further guidance that explains how each of these assessments fulfil risk management requirements established in the Rules, and specifically, to what extent risk assessments should focus on fraud and corruption risks given the parallel work line ministries do to conduct the ITA. In addition, as noted, the internal audit function should not lead risk assessments, in line with international standards, and this can include corruption and fraud risk assessments. Additional guidance from the CGD, the NACC and the PACC could address the following issues:

- Clarify the strategic and operational importance of risk assessments, including an explicit reference to managing fraud and corruption risks. The CGD should communicate that the ITA should not be a substitute for risk assessments at an institutional or operational level that support managers to make decisions about control activities and mitigation measures, as required in the Rules. Separate from the ITA, risk assessments should take into account fraud and corruption risks that could affect the achievement of the agency's objectives.

- Clarify the roles and responsibilities specific to integrity risk management. This could include clarifying the roles and responsibilities of managers for risk management and internal control, as discussed in the previous section. In addition, it could include clarifications about the roles and responsibilities of the internal audit function, the NACC and the PACC, including its network of Anti-Corruption Centres, in the context of risk management requirements. Involving the latter can help to promote risk management at the regional level, which Thai officials highlighted as an ongoing challenge. Moreover, further CGD guidance could clarify the expectations of managers to co-ordinate and benefit from the internal audit function's risk assessments as an input into their own risk management plans and activities.

- Clarify the purpose and use of the results of the ITA relative to integrity risk assessments that managers or internal audit functions may conduct. The ITA serves as a comprehensive, high-level self-assessment tool and means for raising awareness about key integrity issues. However, it is not clear how the government uses the results of the ITA, and whether there are linkages between the ITA and ongoing risk management activities at an operational level. Moreover, any additional guidance or promotional materials that convey the importance of risk management and risk assessments should be cautious about creating causal linkages with Transparency International's Corruption Perception Index (CPI), as described in the previous section. Instead, the guidance can reiterate the benefits of risk management as an approach for navigating uncertainty and driving policy results rather than a means for complying with regulations.

Additional guidance from the CGD can also serve as an opportunity to showcase positive examples across government related to risk management and internal control in the promotion of a race-to-the-top. For instance, every year, the NACC has awarded organisations in the public sector for their contributions and success in launching proactive measures to combat corruption and conduct the ITA, including a ranking of ministries that are top performers. In addition, each year the Office of the Public Sector Development Commission (OPDC) offers a Public Sector Excellence Award (PSEA). In 2017, the OPDC awarded a PSEA to the Department of Rural Roads in the Ministry of Transport for excellence in strategic planning and efficient implementation of the organisation strategy, which included effective risk management and internal control. Additional guidance can showcase such efforts to motivate improvements to integrity risk management and internal control, and more generally a culture of risk that promotes value-based, coherent risk management policies and practices.

Strengthen capacity and knowledge for assessing and managing risks at the regional level

Thailand is a unitary country with three levels to the state administration structure, including central, provincial and local administrations (see Box 2.3 for additional details). The CGD and other bodies, including the PACC and the NACC, have subnational offices that carry out the mandate of the institutions at the regional level. The CGD has 76 offices in the provinces. The ACOCs also have a presence in 76 provinces. In 2018, the OECD recommended the government of Thailand to increase the capacity of the ACOCs. Capacity remains an issue at the provincial level, not only for the ACOCs, but also for the CGD and line ministries with a regional presence, according to Thai officials. In particular, a key area for improvement highlighted by government officials is the capacity of local governments and regional representation of the CGD, the NACC and the PACC to implement reforms for improving integrity risk management and control.

Box 2.3. Organisation of the government in Thailand at the regional level

The 1991 State Administration Act sets out three levels of state administration in Thailand: central, provincial and local. There are 76 provinces nationwide, each supported by a provincial office headed by a provincial governor. The provincial governor is appointed by the central government, except in the Bangkok Metropolitan Administration (BMA), where residents directly elect their governor. Governors are usually officials from the Ministry of Interior and are responsible for implementing central government policies. Provinces are then organised into 928 districts, with 7 416 sub-districts and 61 032 villages. The Ministry of Interior's Department of Provincial Administration appoints the districts' chief officers. Sub-district heads are generally chosen from among the village heads in each sub-district, and village heads are elected by their constituents. Both sub-district and village heads fall under the direct guidance and supervision of provincial governors and chief district officers, who are under central government control.

Thailand's local administration is based on a two-tier system comprising 76 Provincial Administrative Organisations (PAOs), 2 441 municipalities, 5 333 Sub-district Administrative Organisations (SAOs), and two special Local Administrative Organisations (BMA and Pattaya City). PAOs function as the upper tier of the local administration and operate large-scale administrative duties and public services. Municipalities and SAOs constitute the lower tier and are responsible for small-scale duties. Municipalities govern urban areas, while SAOs govern rural areas. There are three types of municipalities: cities (50 000 inhabitants or more), towns (10 000 to 49 999 inhabitants) and townships (7 000 to 9 999 inhabitants).

Provincial governors and chief district officers oversee local administrators to ensure central government policy directives are followed. This leaves limited discretion for PAOs, municipalities and SAOs to determine how funds are spent. However, the Decentralisation Act (1999) aimed to create institutional space for citizens to track and monitor the provision of public services and take part in decision making. In the following years, the direct election of local administrators has been gradually introduced. In 2014, local elections were temporarily suspended in the aftermath of the political crisis

Source: OECD (2018[7]), *Multi-dimensional Review of Thailand (Volume 1): Initial Assessment.*

In interviews, government officials highlighted ongoing challenges facing local administrative agencies to conduct risk assessments and establish effective internal control systems. Officials declared there was no guidance for provincial government entities. This has led to a wide variation and lack of coherence with regard to how local governments approach internal control and risk management. Across all provinces, capacity is low for implementing recent reforms.

The CGD can take the lead to address capacity issues and improve the coherence of approaches to internal control and risk management at the regional level. The aforementioned guidance can address this issue directly, with considerations and support that is tailored to the maturity levels of local administrations. The CGD is already conducting trainings for provincial government entities on risk management, according to officials. Further guidance can provide greater clarity as to how local entities can comply with new reforms. Going beyond that, guidance can add clarity and help to build capacity related to key areas communicated to the OECD in interviews, including: the roles and responsibilities of local government entities for managing risks; methodologies for assessing risks that are commensurate with skill levels and resources; and good practices for using the results of risk assessments.

Enhancing monitoring and evaluation, as well as quality assurance assessments

Develop plans for monitoring and evaluation of internal control and risk management with a specific focus to safeguard integrity in government

International standards emphasise the need for governments to monitor and evaluate the internal control system, and in particular, to assess outcomes and update activities to improve fraud and corruption risk management (COSO, 2016[8]). The OECD's Recommendation on Public Integrity also highlights the need for governments to build efficient monitoring and quality assurance mechanisms for safeguarding integrity in the public sector. Thailand's regulations echo these standards. For instance, Thailand's *Risk Management Standards and Practical Rules for State Agencies* say that heads of agencies should monitor and evaluate risk management activities to ensure the agency adheres to standards and the IIA's Three Lines Model. In addition, government agencies are subject to reporting requirements to ensure they have internal control systems in place and consider risks.

Thailand's reporting requirements include a a "Certificate of Internal Control Assessment," which is a self-assessment report that indicates a public entity has assessed whether internal controls are compliant with the Rule of the Ministry of Finance on Standards and Internal Control Practice for Government Agency B.E. 2561 (2018). As part of this internal control assessment, line ministries must also highlight improvements to internal control activities based on perceived risks. This certificate is the only requirement for public entities to monitor, evaluate and report on M&E of the internal control system. There are other bodies that support these efforts, including a Committee within the CGD that consists of internal auditors as well as financial and compliance auditors of the State Audit Office (SAO). However, the primary responsibility for M&E of the internal control system is within line ministries, in accordance with Thailand's standards.

In principle, the certifications and their underlying assessments can be useful mechanisms for monitoring and evaluating the internal control system in the Thai government. However, the quality and effectiveness of these efforts depend on the methodology, scope and frequency of monitoring, which is not prescribed and is therefore inconsistent from one line ministry to the next. The Certificates promote monitoring and evaluation of the general existence of an internal control structure, and to some extent risks, but there are more determinants of the quality of an internal control system beyond these factors. Box 2.4 provides an example from guidance produced for the United States Agency for International Development (USAID) as part of a toolkit for managers in the health sector, but with broader lessons that are applicable to self-assessment methodologies for internal control.

Box 2.4. USAID: Example of an internal control self assessment in the health sector

Engaging stakeholders across three stages of the self-assessment process

Employing a self-assessment methodology can help instil a level of ownership of both the review process and the findings. It can also aid with internal communication. Communication to internal stakeholders ideally takes place at three stages of the self-assessment process:

1. **Design**: An initial meeting or workshop with officials from throughout the organisation to launch the assessment is important in establishing transparent communication about the assessment process and potential results. The meeting/workshop should be designed to encourage feedback from participants on the assessment design, which would further increase buy-in from internal stakeholders. During this meeting, participants can be provided with talking points to share with their colleagues.

2. **Implementation**: During the self-assessment, the team should be prepared to engage with colleagues about internal controls. The review is an opportunity to engage a broad set of stakeholders on the importance of internal controls, factors that make a good internal control and the findings from the data collection effort. This is particularly important in assessing the difference between practice and policy.

3. **Results**: The results of the assessment need to be communicated clearly and transparently. Senior leadership should focus on prioritising the actionable steps to be taken to strengthen internal control weaknesses, and highlighting those areas where management systems or procedures are not working. Sharing broadly with other staff is important to build accountability for improving internal controls and management systems.

Overview of an output of a self-assessment process

- **Background** - Detailing the context in which the assessment is taking place, major changes or initiatives to address internal controls, the scope and scale of the assessment, and the description of the departments and units being reviewed.

- **Objectives** - Stating the rationale for the self-assessment and the intended use of the findings.

- **Methodology** - Describing the specific scope of the assessment team, the justification for selection of the specific indicators, and the sampling methodology for data collection subnational and facility-level entities.

- **Strengths** - Summarising the areas where internal controls are sufficient, and how that assessment was made.

- **Weaknesses** - Detailing the areas where internal controls are insufficient or weak, and how that assessment was made.

- **Change over time** - If the assessment is being completed regularly, identifying any significant changes, either positive or negative.

- **Next steps** - Describing how the results of the self-assessment will be used to inform efforts to strengthen internal controls.

Source: Long, B. and J. Kanthor (2013[9]), *Self-Assessment of Internal Control Health Care: A Toolkit for Managers*.

Above all, M&E should support public entities in obtaining a better understanding of implementation challenges or vulnerabilities on an ongoing basis. Managers in public entities can conduct M&E in regular intervals and incorporate the results into the reporting process for the Certificates. Risk assessments are not a substitute for M&E. The monitoring and review of risk management processes is a distinct activity from M&E and assessing the quality of internal control systems as a whole, even though these activities may inform each other. For instance, the results of fraud and corruption risk assessments (i.e. the perceived likelihood and impact of the effect of fraud and corruption on objectives) can be one of several factors that help manager's to set priorities for broader M&E activities and quality assessments. Other considerations for prioritising M&E activities include the following:

- objectives and the scope of activities of the public organisation
- issues identified and recommendations of internal and external auditors
- issues identified by the Ministry of Finance or CGD in their role of providing general oversight of the financial operations of line ministries
- results of previous M&E activities or quality assessments
- proportion of irregular expenditure within the overall budget of the public organisation (Boryczka, Bochnar and Larin, 2019[2]).

In the integrity context, the unit of analysis for M&E is not just individual risks, but other governance and institutional factors that determine the effectiveness of the internal control system. Specifically, M&E involves the systematic collection of evidence dealing with the design, implementation and results of the policies, controls and actions taken to manage fraud and corruption risks. Effective monitoring allows managers to adapt controls when issues arise, and evaluations can offer insights into an ongoing or completed activity, to support decisions about relevance, effectiveness and potential alternatives. The current M&E activities related to internal control and risk management help to promote awareness of this critical component of standards, like COSO and Thai's own regulations, but the Certificate process facilitates a check-the-box exercise for line ministries. As a result, there is a danger of government officials perceiving internal control and risk management as compliance activities. In contrast, M&E should facilitate manager's decisions and understanding of the effectiveness of the internal control system, based on evidence of how well measures to safeguard integrity are producing results and advancing organisational objectives.

Ensure the independence and objectivity of quality assurance assessments

As part of its monitoring and evaluation activities, the CGD developed a quality assurance assessment framework for the internal audit function in the public sector. The framework is structured according to international standards of the Institute of Internal Auditors (IIA) and the IIA's International Professional Practices Framework (IPPF), as well as the Principle of Total Quality Management (TQM) and the Deming Management Cycle. It covers four main areas of activity of the internal audit function—governance, staff, management and process—as shown in Table 2.2.

Table 2.2. Thailand's internal audit quality assurance criteria for the public sector

Internal audit activity	Items	IPPF Standards
Governance	1. Structure and reporting lines	1110 Organisational Independence 1120 Individual Objectivity 1130 Impairment to Independence or Objectivity
	2. Internal Audit Charter	1010 Recognising Mandatory Guidance in the Internal Audit Charter
	3. Assessing the quality of the internal audit work	1310 Requirements of the Quality Assurance and Improvement Programme 1320 Reporting on the Quality Assurance and Improvement Programme
	4. Expertise in internal audit	1210 Proficiency
	5. Carefulness as a professional	1220 Due Professional Care
Staff	6. Personnel development	1230 Continuing Professional Development
	7. Strategy of the internal audit department	2030 Resource Management
	8. Risk assessment for audit plan	2010 Planning
Management	9. Audit planning	2020 Communication and Approval
	10. Policy, Operation manual and co-ordination	2040 Policies and Procedures 2050 Co-ordination and Reliance
	11. Internal Audit Report Summary Report	2060 Reporting to Senior Management and the Board 2070 External Service Provider and Organizational Responsibility for Internal Auditing
	12. Operations cover the regulatory process, Risk management and control	2210 Engagement Objectives 2220 Engagement Scope 2230 Engagement Resource Allocation 2240 Engagement Work Programme
	13. Field inspection operations	2310 Identifying Information 2320 Analysis and Evaluation 2330 Documenting Information 2340 Engagement Supervision
Process	14. Report of the audit performance	2410 Criteria for Communicating 2420 Quality of Communications 2430 Use of "Conducted in Conformance with the International Standards for the Professional Practice of Internal Auditing" 2440 Disseminating Results 2450 Overall Opinions
	15. Monitoring results	2500 Monitoring Progress 2600 Communicating the Acceptance of Risks

Source: Developed by the OECD based on documentation provided by CGD and (IIA, 2017[10])

Values for the assessment are attributed at three levels: at the "item" level, the level of the internal audit activity and the overall assessment results. The performance of each item is rated on a scale of 0 to 4, where 0 stands for no action taken and 4 for complete conformity with the established criteria. The points received for each item under the internal audit activity assessed (i.e. governance, staff, management, process) are calculated together to end up with an average score. In the end, the average score is weighted for each internal audit activity. All weighted average scores are added together to reach the overall evaluation score following again a scale of 0 to 4 (where 0-1.99 stands for "does not conform" 2-2.99 stands for "partially conforms" and 3-4 for "generally conforms").

Thailand's quality assurance process includes both quantitative and qualitative criteria depending on the content of each assessment. For example, item 4 on "Expertise in internal audit" uses mostly quantitative indicators such as the percentage of staff with more than 3 years' experience in internal audit and the percentage of certified internal auditors. In comparison, item 8 on "Risk assessment for audit planning" focuses on qualitative indicators related to the risk assessment process, such as coverage of risk factors, use of risk assessment results for audit planning and ability to adjust risk factors depending on the circumstances (Comptroller General's Department, 2016[11]). Using mixed types of indicators is a recommended approach that helps capture and measure the various aspects contributing to the improvement of the internal audit function as a whole.

The CGD's quality assurance assessment aligns with the goals set forth in IIA's Standard 1300, Quality Assurance and Improvement Programme (QAIP), which states, "The chief audit executive must develop and maintain a quality assurance and improvement programme that covers all aspects of the internal audit activity" (IIA, 2017[12]) QAIPs help internal auditors to assess the efficiency and effectiveness of their work and identify areas of improvement. Moreover, they can facilitate a better understanding of risks and performance indicators, thereby aiding decision making and implementation of strategies, policies and procedures. The following are common focus areas of QAIPs:

- Conformance with the definition of internal auditing, the code of ethics, and the standards, including timely corrective actions to remedy non-conformance.
- Adequacy of the internal audit activity's charter, goals, objectives, policies, and procedures.
- Contributions to the organisation's governance, risk management, and control processes.
- Compliance with applicable laws, regulations, and other government standards.
- Effectiveness of continuous improvement activities and adoption of best practices (OECD, 2018[13]).

The CGD's Internal Audit Quality Assessment is described as a collection of information about the internal audit function of government agencies. The CGD identifies the government agencies participating in the quality assurance process. After receiving relevant notice, the heads of the participating government agencies inform the internal audit function, which is asked to complete a self-assessment form and provide all supporting documents and evidence. Examples of supporting documents used in the assessment include the annual audit plan, the code of ethics, audit reports, the internal audit charter and training plans. As a next step, the CGD assesses the quality of the internal audit function based on the established criteria and the evidence provided. During this process, the internal audit function of the participating agencies continues to support the CGD providing additional information and explanations, as necessary. Finally, the quality assessment results are analysed and reported to a committee that consists of CGD officials, as well as senior experts from the private sector, called the Public Sector Quality Assurance Committee.

As described, a key characteristic throughout Thailand's quality assurance assessment of the internal audit function is the heavy involvement of the CGD itself. The CGD, as the central institution monitoring the internal audit function in the public sector, plays a key role in ensuring its quality. While the Public Sector Quality Assurance Committee certifies the results of the assessments, concerns about independence remain. An analogous approach is followed in some EU member countries (European Commission, 2014[14]), reflecting the tasks of central harmonisation units (CHUs) that are similar to the CGD. CHUs can go beyond overseeing, monitoring and advising public sector internal audit functions, and they may conduct external assessments of the internal audit activities of operational units. This practice has raised concerns with regards to the independence and "externality" of the CHU vis-à-vis the internal audit functions under assessment.

In 2012, the European Commission issued an opinion that stated if a CHU's assessment is the only one carried out, it does not satisfy the requirements of IIA's Standards.[4] According to the Commission, despite being a distinct organisational structure, the CHU's assessment should not be considered as both external and independent in line with Standard 1312, since the CHU provides the internal audit activity with assistance and professional guidance (European Commission, 2014[14]). To address this issue, the United

Kingdom, for instance, completely outsourced its external quality assurance assessments, which are carried out by an independent contractor as described in Box 2.5 (U.K. HM Treasury, 2013[15]).

Box 2.5. Assessing audit quality and improving performance of internal audit in the United Kingdom

Internal audit functions at central, devolved and local government levels in the United Kingdom, apply a common set of Public Sector Internal Audit Standards based on the IIA's global standards for the profession. Performance and audit quality are evaluated using a standardised approach, the Internal Audit Quality Assessment Framework.

The Framework is designed to focus on outcomes that improve the effectiveness of internal audit activity and as a result help institutions better meet public service delivery commitments. This tool is used in periodic self-assessments and in external reviews performed by assessors from outside the organisation to embed a common understanding of quality and continuous improvement. The Framework is divided into four key sections with measures of effective performance that go beyond compliance with professional standards:

- **Purpose and positioning**: Does the function have a clear mandate, appropriate status and independence to perform its duties?
- **Structure and resources**: Does the function have access to the relevant technical skills, adequate staffing and sufficient budget to deliver its mandate?
- **Audit execution**: Does the function have adequate policies and processes in place to deliver its mandate effectively and efficiently?
- **Impact**: Does the function have a positive impact on the organisation's ability to deliver its objectives and foster good governance, risk management and control?

Statements of good practice for each measure serve both as a guide to reviewers in applying the Framework and as a roadmap for internal audit functions on specific actions to improve performance. The Framework provides a snapshot of overall effectiveness of the audit function and builds on the results of the most recent internal review to evaluate audit quality over time.

Independence and objectivity of external quality assessments

Internal audit functions are required to have their activity reviewed by an independent assessor at least once every five years. Independence is defined as not having an actual or perceived conflict of interest and not being a part of, or under the control of the organisation of the internal audit function. Audit and risk committees oversee selection of the independent assessment team and the scope of the review.

Source: UK HM Treasury, (2013[15]), Internal Audit Quality Assessment Framework; HM Treasury (2013), External Quality Assessment Specification; Relevant Internal Audit Standard Setters, (2017), Public Sector Internal Audit Standards: Applying the IIA International Standards to the UK Public Sector.

In addition to full external assessments, the CGD could consider other ways to improve the independence of its quality assurance assessments for the internal audit function. For instance, it could create firewalls within its institution to ensure dedicated personnel focus entirely on the quality assessments of the internal audit function. This could be part of or in addition to CGD's own internal audit function. For instance, Peru's Office of the Comptroller General (*Contraloría General de la República*, or CGR) uses an evaluation system for assessing the maturity of internal control components. The independence and "externality" of the evaluator are also crucial in this case. Currently, the CGR has a department of internal control that is primarily responsible for assessing the degree and maturity of the internal control components within public entities (OECD, 2017[16]). Thailand could consider a similar approach in order to further ensure the independence and objectivity of its assessments.

Proposals for action

Enhance the focus on integrity in standards and rules, and clarify roles and responsibilities within the internal control system.

- The CGD could amend the Rules to include a specific reference to integrity risks, linking to institutional objectives, to avoid artificially separating this type of risk from the broader policies, practices and tools used to assess risk management in general.
- The CGD could amend standards or provide additional guidance to further clarify the role of the internal audit function (i.e. the third line) for integrity risk management vis-à-vis managers in government (i.e. the first line).
- The CGD could consider improving self-assessment tools to further promote responsibility, accountability and the authority of managers with regards to internal control and risk management.

Refine communication strategies to demonstrate the added value of risk management for safeguarding integrity and improving governance

- The CGD, along with the NACC, the PACC and leadership of line ministries, can enhance future guidance and communications about risk management and control by having coherent messages that promote managerial ownership and risk management as a tool for better governance.
- The CGD, the NACC and the PACC can enhance guidance with positive messages that emphasise a perspective on risk management and control that is oriented towards governance and achieving the results of policies and goals, rather than compliance with laws and standards.
- The CGD, the NACC and the PACC also can adapt messages about the value of risk management and risk assessments by avoiding causal linkages to improvements in Transparency International's CPI. It is not possible to use the CPI as a tool to measure the performance of specific internal control or risk management activities.

Improve risk management guidance, including clarifying the purpose of different types of risk assessments

- The CGD, in co-ordination with the NACC and the PACC, can offer further guidance that explains how each of these assessments fulfil risk management requirements established in the Rules to ensure consistency and harmonisation across entities. This can include additional guidance at the institutional level to demonstrate how risk assessments should focus on fraud and corruption risks, given the parallel work line ministries do to conduct the ITA.
- Clarify the strategic and operational importance of risk assessments, including an explicit reference to managing fraud and corruption risks. Although CGD does not set the rules for the ITA, the CGD could communicate that the ITA should not be a substitute for risk assessments at an institutional or operational level, as required in the Rules.
- Clarify the purpose and use of the results of the ITA relative to integrity risk assessments that managers or internal audit functions may conduct.

- Use the guidance as an opportunity to showcase positive examples across government related to risk management and internal control to reinforce international standards and good practices, and promote a culture of integrity.

Strengthen capacity and knowledge for assessing and managing risks at the regional level

- The CGD can take the lead to address capacity issues and improve the coherence of approaches to internal control and risk management at the regional level, including additional guidance and trainings that provide greater clarity and knowledge as to how local entities can better manage risks and comply with new reforms.
- Capacity-building efforts at the regional level can focus on key areas identified during the review, including 1) clarity about the roles and responsibilities of local government entities for managing risks; 2) methodologies for assessing risks that are commensurate with skill levels and resources; and 3) good practices for using the results of risk assessments.

Develop plans for monitoring and evaluation of internal control and risk management with a specific focus on safeguarding integrity in government

- The CGD and line ministries could enhance M&E to better understand implementation challenges and vulnerabilities in the integrity system on an ongoing basis. Managers in line ministries can conduct M&E in regular intervals and incorporate the results into the reporting process for Certificates.
- When conducting M&E, the CGD and line ministries can focus on assessing governance and institutional factors that determine the effectiveness of the internal control system in addition to risks. This additional element can help to ensure that M&E is not just a check-the-box exercise with risk assessments.

Ensure the independence and objectivity of the quality assurance assessment

- The CGD could consider to improve the independence and objective of its quality assurance assessments for the internal audit function, such as creating firewalls between teams to ensure dedicated personnel focus entirely on the quality assessments of the internal audit function.

References

Boryczka, M., D. Bochnar and A. Larin (2019), "Guidelines for assessing the quality of internal control systems", *SIGMA Papers*, No. 59, OECD Publishing, Paris, https://dx.doi.org/10.1787/2a38a1d9-en.   [2]

Comptroller General's Department (2016), *Criteria for quality assurance of internal audit in the public sector*.   [11]

COSO (2016), *Fraud Risk Management Guide*, Committee of Sponsoring Organizations of the Treadway Commission, https://www.coso.org/Pages/Purchase-Guide.aspx (accessed on 13 September 2020).   [8]

European Commission (2014), *Public Internal Control Systems in the European Union Quality Assurance for Internal Audit*, https://ec.europa.eu/budget/pic/lib/docs/pic_paper3_en.pdf.   [14]

Government of Thailand (2017), *Master Plan under the National Strategy on Anti-Corruption and Misconduct*.   [4]

IIA (2017), *International Standards for the Professional Practice of Internal Auditing*, The Institute of Internal Auditors Research Foundation, https://na.theiia.org/standards-guidance/Public%20Documents/IPPF-Standards-2017.pdf.   [10]

IIA (2017), *Quality Assessment Manual for the Internal Audit Activity*, The Institute of Internal Auditors Research Foundation, https://global.theiia.org/standards-guidance/topics/Pages/Quality-Assessment-Manual.aspx.   [12]

Long, B. and J. Kanthor (2013), *Self-Assessment of Internal Control Health Care: A Toolkit for Managers*, United States Agency for International Development, Health Finance & Governance Project, Abt Associates Inc., https://www.hfgproject.org/toolkit-ministries-health-work-effectively-ministries-finance/.   [9]

Ministry of Finance (2018), *B.E. 2561: Internal Audit Standards and Ethics for Internal Auditing of Government Agencies*.   [1]

National Economic and Social Development Council of Thailand (2019), *Fraud risk management plan for fiscal year 2019*.   [5]

OECD (2018), *Internal Audit Manual for the Greek Public Administration*, OECD Public Governance Reviews, OECD Publishing, Paris, https://dx.doi.org/10.1787/9789264309692-en.   [13]

OECD (2018), *Multi-dimensional Review of Thailand (Volume 1): Initial Assessment*, OECD Development Pathways, OECD Publishing, Paris, https://dx.doi.org/10.1787/9789264293311-en.   [7]

OECD (2018), *OECD Integrity Review of Thailand: Towards Coherent and Effective Integrity Policies*, OECD Public Governance Reviews, OECD Publishing, Paris, https://dx.doi.org/10.1787/9789264291928-en.   [6]

OECD (2017), *OECD Integrity Review of Peru: Enhancing Public Sector Integrity for Inclusive Growth*, OECD Public Governance Reviews, OECD Publishing, Paris, https://dx.doi.org/10.1787/9789264271029-en.   [16]

The Dutch Ministry of Finance (March 2018), *Good Financial Governance and Public Internal Control, Presentation to the OECD.* [3]

The Office of the National Anti-Corruption Commission (2019), *Integrity and Transparency Assessment*, https://itas.nacc.go.th/file/download/113259. [17]

U.K. HM Treasury (2013), *Internal Audit Quality Assessment Framework*, https://assets.publishing.service.gov.uk/government/uploads/system/uploads/attachment_dat a/file/204214/internal_audit_quality_assessment_framework.pdf. [15]

Notes

[1] Principle 10 of the OECD's Recommendation on Public Integrity focuses on the following objectives: 1) ensuring a control environment with clear objectives that demonstrate managers' commitment to public integrity and public-service values, and that provides a reasonable level of assurance of an organisation's efficiency, performance and compliance with laws and practices; 2) ensuring a strategic approach to risk management that includes assessing risks to public integrity, addressing control weaknesses (including building warning signals into critical processes) as well as establishing an efficient monitoring and quality assurance mechanism for the risk management system; 3) ensuring control mechanisms are coherent and include clear procedures for responding to credible suspicions of violations of laws and regulations, and facilitating reporting to the competent authorities without fear of reprisal.

[2] As of April 2020, the IIA is the process of revising its Three Lines of Defense Model, including changing the name to the Three Lines Model and considering its applicability to the public sector. See the IIA's website (http://bit.ly/39Y3QT1) for additional information.

[3] The three surveys conducted for the ITA include the following: 1) the Internal Integrity and Transparency Assessment, a self-assessment to gather employees' perceptions about organisational culture and management; 2) the External Integrity and Transparency Assessment, an external survey focused on organisational reputation and stakeholders' perceptions about performance; and 3) the Open Data Integrity and Transparency Assessment, an evidence-based survey that assesses the organisation's open data activities through reviews of websites and online publications. In general, the ITA covers 10 topics for each organisational assessment, including: 1) performance effectiveness; 2) efficiency and transparency of performance budgeting; 3) legitimacy and use of powers; 4) efficiency and integrity for use of public assets and properties; 5) effectiveness of corruption mitigation measures; 6) quality of operations; 7) communications effectiveness; 8) effectiveness of performance improvement; 9) transparency of public data; and 10) corruption prevention (The Office of the National Anti-Corruption Commission, 2019[17]). The Integrity and Transparency Assessment System (ITAS) supports the data collection for the ITA to ensure timely and consistent assessments across entities.

[4] Opinion of 13 November 2012 of the Commission's Directorate-General for Budget addressed to the CHUs of (potential) candidate countries, qualifying European Neighbourhood Policy countries and delegates in the Public Expenditure Management Peer Assisted Learning (PEMPAL) organisation.

3 Ensuring transparency and integrity in Thailand's public decision making

This chapter provides an assessment of policies that aim to promote transparency and integrity in public decision making in the Kingdom of Thailand. It identifies weaknesses in the current legal framework, such as the lack of specific guidelines or regulations on how stakeholders and public officials interact during policy making. Furthermore, it raises practical concerns related to the enforcement and implementation of the regulations in place such as the lack of data and broad assessments on public consultations. Based on the analysis and the Recommendation of the OECD Council on Public Integrity, the chapter provides recommendations to foster regulations on stakeholder engagement and participation in policy making, for example by developing rules for interactions between stakeholders and public officials. Further, it provides advice to promote transparency and access to information on decision making, as well as to strengthen enforcement by raising awareness and including sanctions in regulations.

Introduction

Inclusive public policies and decision making based on integrity, participation and transparency legitimise and make policies more effective, thereby strengthening citizens' trust in governments (OECD, 2017[1]). However, powerful individuals and interest groups can use their wealth, power or advantages to tip the scale in their favour at the expense of the public interest. When public policy decisions are consistently or repeatedly directed away from the public interest towards the interests of a specific interest group or persons, policies are captured rendering them unfair and exclusive (OECD, 2017[2]). Public policies that systematically favour narrow interest groups could affect the delivery of public services in the long-term, as well as fair competition, trust in government and the legitimacy of political systems.

The OECD Recommendation on Public Integrity (OECD, 2017[3]) states that governments should "encourage transparency and stakeholders' engagement at all stages of the political process and policy cycle to promote accountability and the public interest". Indeed, enforcing the right to know through transparency and access to information, and the inclusive and fair participation of stakeholders are key instruments for levelling the playing field and protecting the policy-making process from being dominated by particular interests.

Over the past decades, Thailand has made impressive economic progress: it has joined the rank of upper middle-income economies, poverty has been reduced, and economic growth and well-being indicators have improved steadily (OECD, 2019[4]). However, data from the World Economic Forum's Global Competitiveness Report 2017-2018 shows that Thailand seems to be, on average, more vulnerable to undue influence than other countries in Southeast Asia and the OECD, exhibiting lower levels of perceived transparency in government policy making (Figure 3.1). Besides, while according to the Asian Development Bank, Thailand shows the lowest levels of reported bribery solicitations in the continent (9.9% of firms in the country reported experiencing bribery requests), the perception among representatives from business reflects that government officials show favouritism to well-connected firms and individuals when deciding upon policies and contracts (IMF, World Economic Outlook Database). Further, country experts from the Varieties of Democracies Project consider that most of Thailand's social and infrastructure spending systematically favours a specific corporation, sector, or set of constituents, instead of allocating social and infrastructure expenditures for the benefit of society as a whole (V-Dem Institute, University of Gothenburg).

Figure 3.1. Undue influence comes along with lower levels of perceived transparency of government policy making

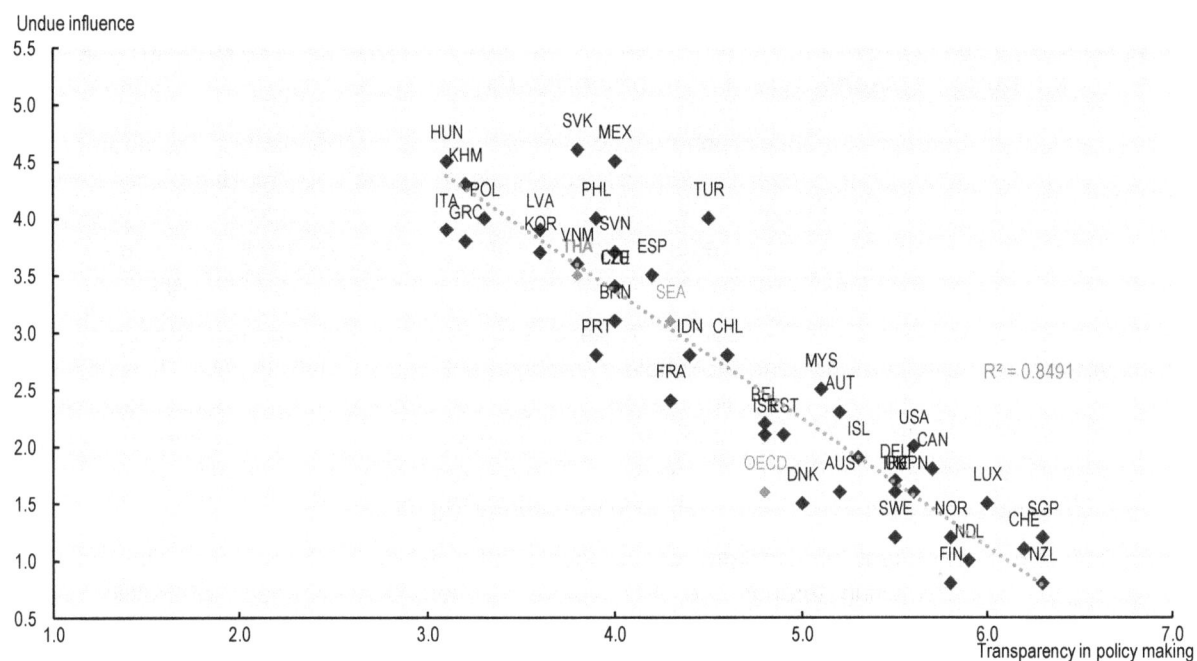

Note: A value of 0 is "low" and a value of 6, "high". The scores for the "undue influence" indicator have been inverted to reflect that higher scores mean higher levels of undue influence. The World Economic Forum calculates the indicator based on the responses to two questions, relating to judicial independence ("In your country, to what extent is the judiciary independent from influences of members of government, citizens, or firms?") and favouritism ("In your country, to what extent do government officials show favouritism to well-connected firms and individuals when deciding upon policies and contracts?"). Level of transparency of government policy making is calculated based on the response to the question "In your country, how easy is it for companies to obtain information about changes in government policies and regulations affecting their activities".
Source: IMF, World Economic Outlook Database 2017.

Promoting integrity and transparency in public policy making is a precondition to building inclusive and fair societies and averting policy capture. An important step in this direction is to implement broader anti-corruption measures, such as the ones in place in Thailand (OECD, 2018[5]). Nonetheless, to ensure that influence on public policies is wielded correctly and to prevent the capture of public policies by private interests, Thailand could increase its efforts to make policy making more accessible, inclusive and accountable to citizens. In particular, this chapter provides recommendations along the following lines of work:

- Fostering regulations on stakeholder engagement and participation in policy making.
- Promoting transparency and access to information on decision making.
- Strengthening enforcement and regulations awareness raising.

Fostering regulations on stakeholder engagement and participation in policy making

Thailand could initiate discussions to develop clear and comprehensive regulations on interactions between stakeholders and public officials

Advocacy and interest groups can bring much-needed information to the policy debate. Transparent and fair competition of interests through legal and legitimate channels during decision-making processes lead to public policies that include constituents' views and concerns, and favour the public interest. However, if there are no effective mechanisms to regulate how private interests influence and interact with policy makers, some interests may have uneven access to decision-making process and capture policies.

Section 77 of the Constitution of the Kingdom of Thailand requires the use of good regulatory practices, such as regulatory impact assessment, stakeholder engagement and ex post reviews. It recognises interactions between stakeholders and policy makers during public decision making, and states that the public and stakeholders should be taken into consideration during law-making processes. In addition, implementing requirements under Section 77, the *Act on Legislative Drafting and Evaluation of Legislation B.E. 2560* (2019) requires the public to be involved in every drafting process.

Furthermore, the government of Thailand encourages public agencies to promote stakeholders' participation in decision making through the "Participatory Governance Category" of Public Sector Excellence Awards. The Office of the Public Sector Development Commission (OPDC) gives this award to government agencies committed to the promotion and development of an effective public administration which meets people's needs on the basis of accountability and public participation.

Yet, there are no specific regulations on how the private and the public sector should actually interact during legislative drafting or broader policy making. As evidenced during the interviews conducted by the OECD in Thailand, no official mechanisms are in place to regulate or prevent big companies from contacting ministers and policy makers privately during policy-making processes. Indeed, uneven access to policy making was also raised as a concern by Thai Civil Society Organisations (CSOs), pointing out that only a few private actors and businesses have access to direct communications with policy makers to influence legislation, policies or administrative decisions (Nimitmongkol, 2019[6]).

The lack of clear stipulations regulating how the private sector is involved in policy making can lead to potential conflicts of interest and may create opportunities for influencing and developing bias in policies. Hence, many OECD countries have either legislative frameworks, rules of procedure or codes of conduct to regulate interactions between stakeholders and public officials and policy makers (Figure 3.2). For example, in Korea, the *Act on the Prevention of Corruption and the Establishment and Management of the Anticorruption and Civil Rights Commission* includes a specific code of conduct for public officials that regulates interactions with private stakeholders. In Italy, the *Rules of procedure of the Parliament* require that everyone who represents an interest, and interacts with policy makers, should register and report their activities, as well as disclose their interests. In France, according to *Law No. 2016-1691 on transparency, the fight against corruption and on the modernisation of economic life*, the High Authority for Transparency in Public Life (HATVP) manages a public register through which citizens can access information about the identity of interest representatives who try to influence policies, the activities they perform in order to influence, the expenditure related to these activities, as well as public decisions targeted by them.

Figure 3.2. Many OECD countries regulate interactions between private stakeholders and policy makers

Number of countries by type of regulation

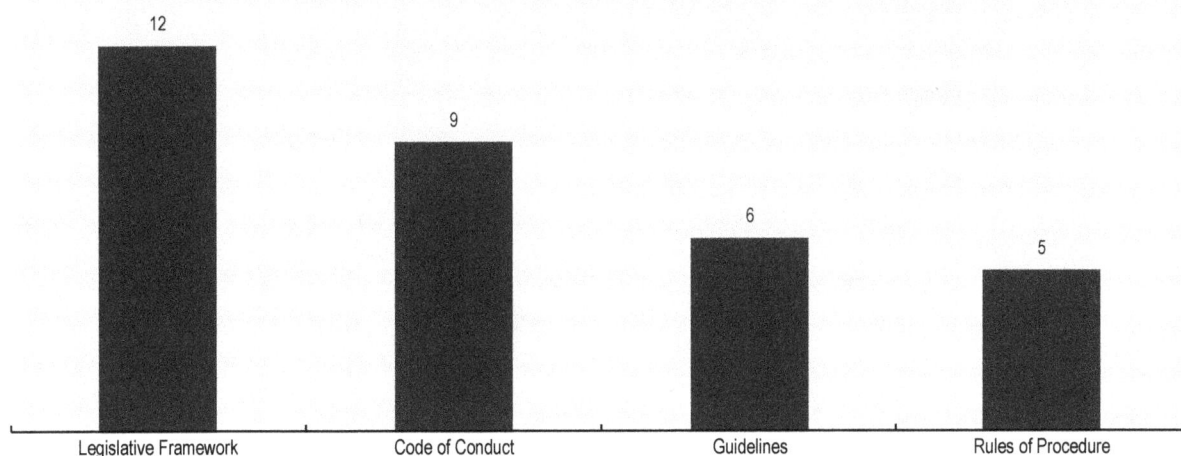

Note: Data is based on 31 OECD member countries.
Source: 2020 OECD Survey on Lobbying.

Following these examples, Thailand could initiate discussions in order to draft specific rules or guidelines to regulate interactions between different stakeholders and public officials during policy making. To ensure policies are made in the public interest and fair interactions during their design, these rules could for example require the disclosure of stakeholders' names and the activities they carry out if they intend to influence policies, or could specify that stakeholders who want to influence policies should be registered.

Alternatively, Thailand could include a directive in the Code of Professional Ethics for the Civil Service or provide a set of rules or principles establishing how public officials and policy makers must be contacted or how they should interact with private stakeholders. For instance, the current drafting of the Code of Conduct for Parliamentarians could be an opportunity to include these dispositions, similar to the one in Spain, which defines the notion of "lobbyist" and establishes an obligation for public officials to disclose information on their meetings with lobbyists. The example of the Code of Conduct for Deputies and Senators in Spain is described in Box 3.1.

Box 3.1. The Code of Conduct for Deputies in Spain

Article 5. Gifts

1. The members of the Parliament shall refrain from accepting, for their own benefit or for their family environment, gifts or gifts of value, favors, services, invitations or trips that are offered by reason of their position or that could be reasonably perceived as an attempt to influence in their conduct as parliamentarians.

2. It is understood included in the previous section that gift, gift or similar benefit that you have an estimated value greater than 150 euros.

3. Members of the Cortes Generales may receive personal gifts from friends and family that have been granted without any connection with their work as parliamentarians. They will also be admissible gifts, discounts, promotions or benefits of a similar nature that are common according to with the uses and customs and whose offer and delivery are unrelated to its activity politics.

4. Gifts and gifts received by a member of the Parliament on official trips of the Chamber or when they act on their behalf, they must be delivered to the Secretariat General of the corresponding Chamber as long as they are offered by reason of said representation and not in a personal capacity and have an estimated value of more than EUR 150. Such gifts will be inventoried and published on the website of the Parliament or Senate.

Article 6. Biographical data and agenda

1. A brief review of the biographical data will be published on the website of the respective Chamber, including information on the personal, academic and professional background of the members of the Parliament. In it you can consult all the titles, data and files that the same parliamentarian considers relevant.

2. Likewise, the members of the Chambers shall make their institutional agenda public in the corresponding Transparency Portal, including in any case the meetings held with the representatives of any entity that has the status of an interest group.

3. For these purposes, and as long as the reform of the Regulations to regulate the Registry and the activity of the interest groups in the Chambers are not forthcoming, will be considered an interest group, lobby or lobbyist: those natural or legal persons or entities without legal personality that communicate directly or indirectly with holders of public or elected positions or their staff in favor of private, public, individual or collective interests, trying to modify or influence issues related to the preparation or modification of legislative initiatives.

4. In both cases, as well as with respect to the declaration of economic interests provided for in the Article 4.3, each parliamentarian will be responsible for the veracity, accuracy and timeliness of the published information.

Source: https://www.congreso.es/public_oficiales/L14/CORT/BOCG/A/BOCG-14-CG-A-70.PDF

Thailand could include specific guidelines on the processes, methods and timeframes for stakeholder engagement in the new Act on Public Consultation

Public policies in the public interest require the development of regulations to ensure not only fair interactions during policy making, but also fair participation, by granting all stakeholders equal access and proactively promoting their engagement. Meaningful stakeholder engagement safeguards the public interest, enhances the inclusiveness of policies, inspires ownership over policy outcomes and stimulates innovative solutions. By involving people in the policy-making process, governments can collect empirical information for analytical purposes, identify policy alternatives, and measure expectations resulting in valuable information on which to base their policy decisions (OECD, 2018[7]). OECD countries make use of a variety of tools to consult, both with the general public and targeted stakeholders (Figure 3.3).

Figure 3.3. Countries engage stakeholders in many ways

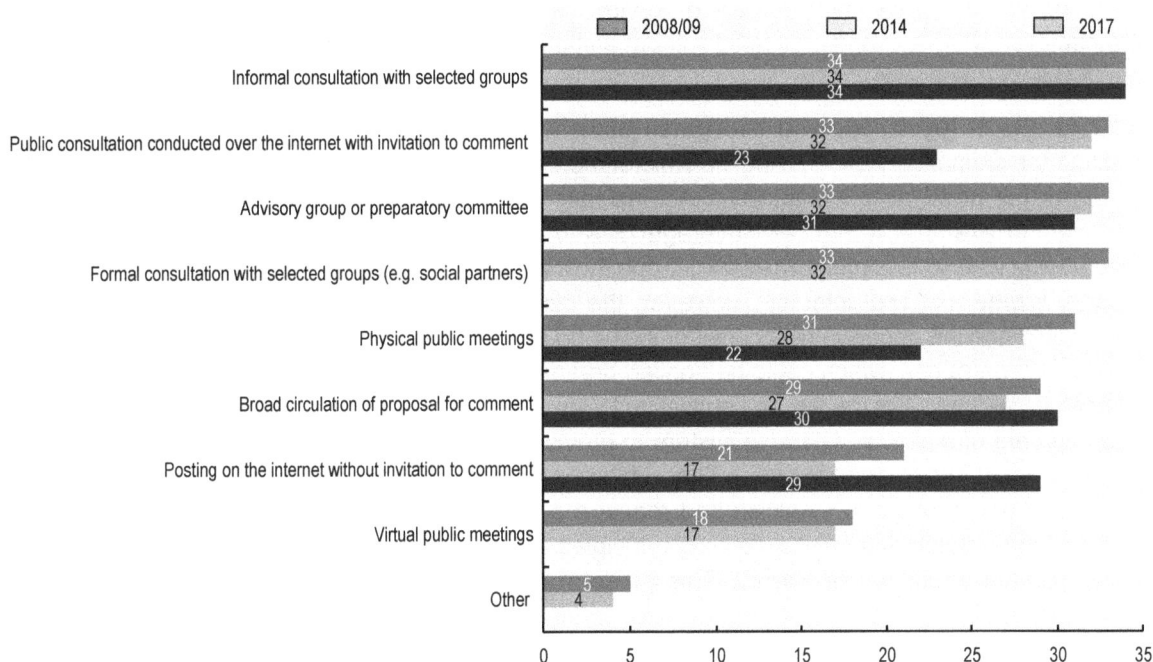

Note: Data is based on 34 OECD member countries and the European Union.
Source: (OECD, 2018[7]).

In Thailand, section 77 of the Constitution of the Kingdom states that prior to the enactment of every law, the State should conduct consultation with stakeholders, analyse any impacts that may occur from the law thoroughly and systematically, and should also disclose the results of the consultation and analysis to the public, and take them into consideration at every stage of the legislative process. Hence, the Act on Legislative Drafting and Evaluation of Legislation B.E. 2560 (2019) includes the requirement for a public consultation before every drafting process begins. Public consultation mechanisms include, among others, meetings, interviews, questionnaires, providing input digitally, or inviting different stakeholders to explain or express their opinions (to learn more about stakeholder engagement see forthcoming OECD Regulatory Reform Review of Thailand).

However, formally requiring stakeholder engagement during policy making is not sufficient to ensure effective implementation: broad and updated information and communication of the processes, as well as the timing and scope of engagement are important considerations. For instance, if engagement procedures do not include all relevant stakeholders, or only engage them after drafts and relevant discussions were developed – that is, in the late stages of policy making – stakeholders are likely to feel de facto excluded from the decision-making process and may abstain from participating in the future.

Additionally, the Rule of the Office of the Prime Minister on Public Consultation B.E. 2548 (2005) states that public consultations are in general optional, and only compulsory if the expected impact on the public is high. This leaves considerable room for discretion to ministries concerning engagement processes. Indeed, a study conducted by the Reform Commission of the Office of the Council of State found that 90%

of Thai legislation related to trade was based on a closed government control system, that consultation was uncommon, and that legal initiatives presented vague, broad subjects which did not address focused or specific topics and did not provide evidence or data for support (Ongkittikul and Thongphat, 2016[8]). Accordingly, stakeholders do not have easy and timely access to all information regarding consultations or are not familiar with the many channels and ways used for engagement. Further, evidence from other OECD governance reviews also points to the fact that public consultation– when carried out –is not dynamic and aims at complying with regulations rather than on extracting value from these exercises (forthcoming OECD Open and Connected Review of Thailand). Consultations often appeared to be announced at short notice, and organised without a standardised protocol (forthcoming OECD Regulatory Reform Review of Thailand).

In order to reform regulations and strengthen stakeholder engagement, the Government of Thailand established the Committee for Revising the Rule of the Office of the Prime Minister on Public Consultation. The draft for the new Public Consultation Act includes some dispositions that are broader than current regulations. For example, it requires State agencies to always disseminate information and consult with affected people whenever a project deals with "quality of environment, health, sanitary condition, the quality of life or any other material interest". However, the disposition is rather vague and the government of Thailand could use the opportunity to consider including specific and detailed guidelines on the processes, methods and timeframes, which could be applied broadly to the general regulatory processes. Moreover, as included in Section 11 of the Act on Legislative Drafting and Evaluation of Legislation B.E. 2560 (2019), the development of a central database system to provide all stakeholders with open, timely and relevant information, would further encourage the Thai citizens' engagement in participation processes. The Digital Government Agency plans to establish and manage a centralised web-portal that will host information prepared by the regulators on the underlying principles and rationale for considered legislative measures even before legal drafting has started. This platform could benefit from some experiences in OECD countries (Box 3.2).

Box 3.2. Online websites on participation and stakeholder engagement

The Scottish government webpage on public consultations

The Scottish Government has a webpage which includes information on all the consultations that have been made and that are open to participation. The website provides an overview and reasons for the consultation, access to the consultation papers and allows for online participation. In addition, the website provides detailed information on past consultations in a user-friendly way, covering the issue for consultation, responses and how the input was used. It presents information on the individual contributions and answers provided for each input. Further, people are able to register for a mailing list, through which they receive information on forthcoming consultations and updates on the ongoing processes.

The Finnish's webpage "Demokratia"

The Ministry of Justice of Finland established "Demokratia", a website presenting all the different channels for influencing public decision making at different territorial levels (including the supranational). It also includes a list of issues that are part of ongoing discussions, with direct links to opportunities for participation. Among the initiatives, there is a nationwide youth advocacy service that allows young people to easily submit suggestions and participate in different consultation processes.

Source: Scottish Government (2020), Scottish Government consultations (website), https://consult.gov.scot/ (accessed on 15 September 2020); Finnish Government (2020), "Discover the different channels for influencing", http://www.demokratia.fi/en/home/www.demokratia.fi/en/home/ (accessed on 15 September 2020).

Promoting transparency and access to information on decision making

Thailand could consider including in the new Official Information Law guidance for citizens requesting public information and a more detailed mandate and requirements for the Information Commission

Transparency has been proven as a key element in anti-corruption policies. It provides people and civil society organisations with the opportunity to monitor and hold public servants and representatives to account. Moreover, there is a strong correlation between public trust in politicians and transparency in government policy making (OECD, 2017[1]). Granting citizens the right to know, and regulations on access to public information are important tools to curb corruption.

Transparency consists of both active and passive actions on the part of the government. On the one hand, governments need to proactively make information public, allowing individuals to access and use this information (active transparency). This includes the publication of open government data by public sector organisations. As discussed in the *OECD Open and Connected Review of Thailand,* this could also help in preventing corruption and policy capture. Section 59 of the Constitution of the Kingdom of Thailand establishes that *the State shall disclose any public data or information in the possession of a State agency, which is not related to the security of the State or government confidentiality*, and shall ensure that the public can conveniently access such information.

On the other hand, transparency is also about responding to requests for information by individuals, e.g. through access to information laws (passive transparency). In Thailand, the right to information is granted through the *Official Information Act B.E 2540* adopted in 1997, and Section 41 of the National Constitution recognises that: "*A person and community shall have the right to be informed and have access to public data or information in possession of a State agency as provided by law*" (Box 3.3).

Box 3.3. Access to information in Thailand

The *Official Information Act B.E 2540* (1997) gives people the opportunity to access broad information about various government operations. It is seen as a precondition for the people to exercise their political rights, as well as to better promote people's interests.

The State bodies liable under the Act include central, provincial and local administrations, state enterprises, professional supervisory organisations, independent agencies of the state and other agencies.

The *Act* details the information that can be accessed, and is disclosed proactively or upon request, such as the authority structure and contact location of government agencies, laws, regulations, cabinet resolutions, plans, projects, annual expenditure budgets, or the results of a decision having a direct effect on the private sector, among others. Any person who deems that a government agency is not disseminating such information has the right to make a complaint to the committee.

Moreover, the *Act* also details the information that cannot be accessed, such as information that causes damage to national security, impairs law enforcement, etc.

In addition to the Official Information Act, there other relevant laws that regulate access to information, including the *Licensing Facilitation Act B.E 2558* (2015) and the *Public Procurement and Supplies Administration Act B.E. 2560 (2017)*. The Licensing Facilitation Act requires government agencies to create and disclose manuals for approval of licenses, which must contain the details about rules, procedures, conditions of documents or evidence used to submit the requests and duration of approval.

The Organic Act on Anti-corruption requires government agencies to disclose information on procurement projects through the electronic channels for public access.

Source: Inputs provided by the Secretariat of the Cabinet and ARTICLE 19 (2015), "The Right to Information in Thailand", https://www.article19.org/resources/the-right-to-information-in-thailand/ (accessed on 15 September 2020).

According to the Global Right to Information Index (RTI), the legal quality of Thailand's Official Information Act –scoring 76 points- is below the OECD average, but slightly above the average score of other South East Asia countries included in the RTI (Figure 3.4).

Figure 3.4. In terms of its legal framework, Thailand's Right to Information regulation is slightly below the OECD average and above the Southeast Asia average

Right to Information Rating 2018

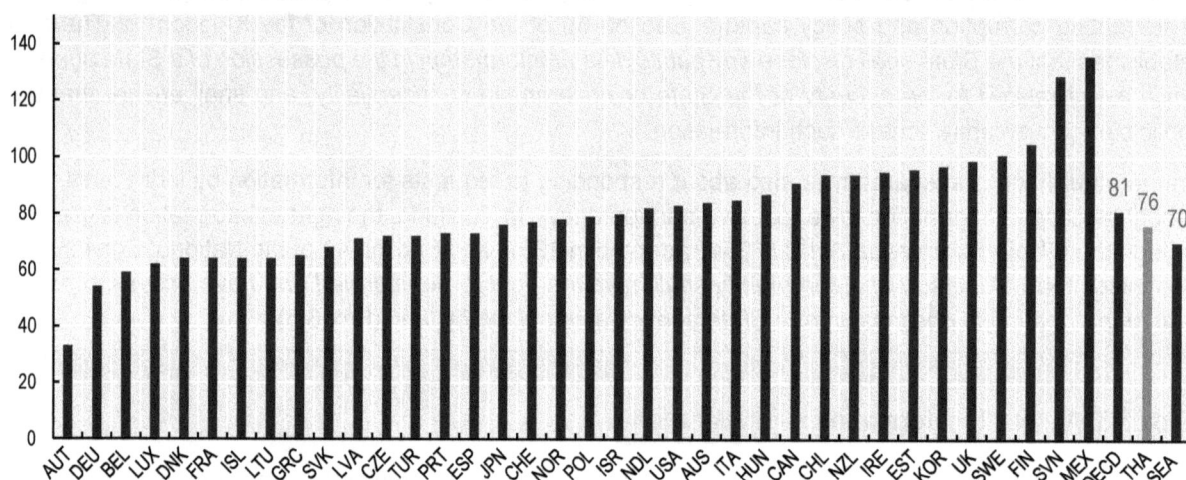

Note: The maximum achievable composite score is 150 and reflects a strong RTI legal framework. The global rating of RTI laws is composed of 61 indicators measuring seven dimensions: Right of access; Scope; Requesting procedures; Exceptions and refusals; Appeals; Sanctions and protection; and Promotional measures. Southeast Asia (SEA) countries are: Brunei, Cambodia, East Timor, Indonesia, Laos, Malaysia, Myanmar (Burma), Philippines, Singapore, Thailand and Vietnam. No data available for Brunei, Cambodia, Laos, Malaysia, Myanmar (Burma) and Singapore.
Source: Access Info Europe (AIE) and the Centre for Law and Democracy (CLD), Right to Information Rating.

In addition to the legal framework and as part of the measures to publish government information, Thailand has created the Government Service Center (GovChannel), which allows the public to access some information online, even if not all government information and data are made accessible on the same website, and multiple exemptions to disclosure remain (Figure 3.5). The platform is a first step to increase discoverability by federating the access to public sector information, data and services through one single domain.

Figure 3.5. Thailand's Government Service Centre website

Source: Thai Government (n.d.), Thailand's Government Service Centre website, www.govchannel.go.th/ (accessed on 15 September 2020).

Thailand's *Official Information Act B.E 2540* (1997) allows people to request official information from a State agency, while protecting individuals' privacy rights and the possibility to express their opinions. However, the law does not provide guidance or detailed procedures to request information. For instance, the law is very vague with regard to deadlines and rules on extension, and the institution receiving requests is not obliged to transfer the request in case information cannot be obtained. Additionally, the Ministry of Interior of Thailand has developed a policy that links data from various government agencies to ID cards, which means citizens can use only their ID card to request information, thus reducing in practice the scope of the regulation that currently applies to all natural persons. These elements could obstruct the implementation of the Act and individuals' actual requests for information, as confirmed by the findings and recommendations on access to information of the forthcoming *Open and Connected Government Review of Thailand*.

In this regard, Thailand could take advantage of current discussions on the Official Information Act reform to include dispositions that could guide citizens requesting public information. In Mexico, for example, the *General Law on Transparency and Access to Public Information* states that all proceedings concerning the right of access to information must be substantiated in a simple and expeditious manner. Any person, by themselves or through a representative, can request access to information via the Transparency Unit, the National Platform, at the office or offices designated for this purpose, via email, mail, courier, verbally or by any means approved by the National System (Article 122, Mexico's *General Law on Transparency and Access to Public Information*).

On the other hand, concerning the mandate and organisation of the Official Information Commission, it has been noted that it has a very small number of staff and approximately convenes three to four times per year. Furthermore, the Commission does not issue binding decisions and does not have a mandate or authority over other agencies. In addition, the Official Information Commissioner –the head of the Commission, who functions as a chairman for the Board - is appointed by the Prime Minister and dependent on the Prime Minister's Office, hence he/she changes when the government does. All these elements affect not only the independence but also performance of the Commission turning the outcomes of their studies and decisions into mere declarative statements with no enforcement power.

In order to ensure an effective implementation of the legislative framework, the government of Thailand may strengthen and further promote the independence of Thailand's Information Commissioner. Effective oversight bodies should be independent from the government, have their own budget and appoint their members based on specific appointing requirements and criteria. In this context, and also as part of the reform of the Official Information Law, Thailand could consider the case of the Information Commission in Indonesia. Commissioners are experts, nominated by the president, but appointed by the Parliament (Articles 30 and 31 of the Public Information Disclosure Act). Further, the Commission's decisions are binding (Articles 39 and 46), it is assigned its own budget and it is able to request additional budget from the Parliament if necessary (Article 29).

Thailand could consider providing a legislative footprint and making legislative discussions open to the public

During the last decade, in parallel with the global decline of trust in governments, an increasing number of countries have introduced tools and regulations to enhance the transparency and integrity of the public decision-making process, for example the disclosure of "legislative footprints" (Figure 3.6). A legislative footprint is a document that details the time, identity and subject of a legislator's contact with a stakeholder (Berg and Freund, 2015[9]). It enables public scrutiny of the entire legislative process. As a way to strengthen transparency, many OECD countries have made public the names of organisations and people who policy makers have met with and consulted while drafting legislation, or those to whom they have disclosed discussions and interventions held within committees and parliamentary bodies (Box 3.4).

Figure 3.6. OECD countries' policies for transparency in policy making

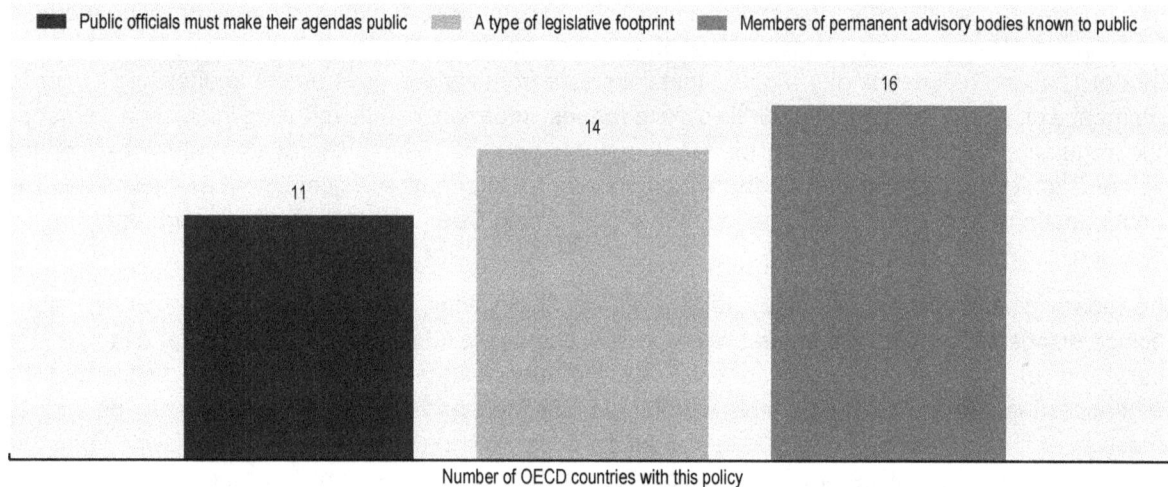

Legend: Public officials must make their agendas public | A type of legislative footprint | Members of permanent advisory bodies known to public

11 | 14 | 16

Number of OECD countries with this policy

Source: OECD PMRI 2018.

Box 3.4 Legislative footprint in Germany

In Germany, federal government decisions are prepared for by way of written cabinet submissions. The covering letters must contain:

- a brief outline of the matter and a statement of the reason for proposing the decision
- details of which federal ministries were involved and with what results
- the results of consultations with associations, particularly their main suggestions
- the outcomes resulting from the input from *Länder* (state) governments and any problems expected – especially if a Bundesrat (parliamentary) procedure is required
- the opinions of the federal government commissioners, federal commissioners, and federal government co-ordinators involved
- the foreseeable costs and budgetary effects of implementing the proposed decision.

Source: (OECD, 2014[10]).

In Thailand, according to Section 77 of the Constitution of the Kingdom of Thailand, the State should ensure that the public has proper access to laws and is able to understand them easily. This is echoed by section 5 of the *Act on Legislative Drafting and Evaluation of Legislation B.E. 2560* (2019), which states that the government shall provide the public easy access to legislation so they can understand and comply with the law correctly. However, the main objective of these dispositions is to underline the responsibility of citizens to comply with legislation by ensuring comprehensibility, rather than to foster transparency in decision making. In this sense, though the public can have access to legislation, they cannot access information on the decision-making processes.

In order to foster citizens' trust in government through transparency, Thailand could therefore provide complete information on different legislative stages and gear the information provided towards promoting transparency in decision-making processes. To this end, the Office of the Council of State is planning to develop a new website and have it ready by the end of 2020. This platform is being designed to support various regulatory policy tools and become the country's central legal database. Meanwhile, as an initial step, the website of the National Assembly could be updated in order to systematise all the available information. In particular, it should be ensured that all links are functioning properly and that all information is presented in a user-friendly way, grouping data by topic, status, etc. Additionally, the Secretariat of the House of Representatives could consider the inclusion of a disposition within legislative regulations making available to the public additional information on the legislative process, similar to the majority of OECD countries. For example, this could include information on discussions in Commissions or Assembly, or meetings with experts and stakeholders.

Thailand may consider requiring policy makers to make their agendas open and accessible to the public

Opening policy makers' agendas could allow individuals and organisations to know which interest representatives or groups have had access to policy makers, and when they have been approached. This could increase transparency with regards to how policy-making processes are influenced by various interests, beyond the legislative processes or safeguards that may already be in place. Further, it could strengthen enforcement of regulations, complementing specific dispositions to promote integrity and avert the capture of decision-making processes.

Indeed, many OECD countries require that public officials that are involved in regulatory processes make their agendas available to the public. In Spain, for example, all members of Government are required to disclose their professional agendas, detailing all their daily meetings. The agendas can be accessed online through the webpages of the entities or through the Official Transparency Platform. In Chile, the Council for Transparency manages an online website, where all the information on public officials' meetings is made public (Box 3.5).

Box 3.5. Online information on public officials' meetings and hearings in Chile

As part of enforcing and implementing *Law No. 20.730*, the Council for Transparency in Chile developed an online platform to give access to data on public officials' hearings and meetings.

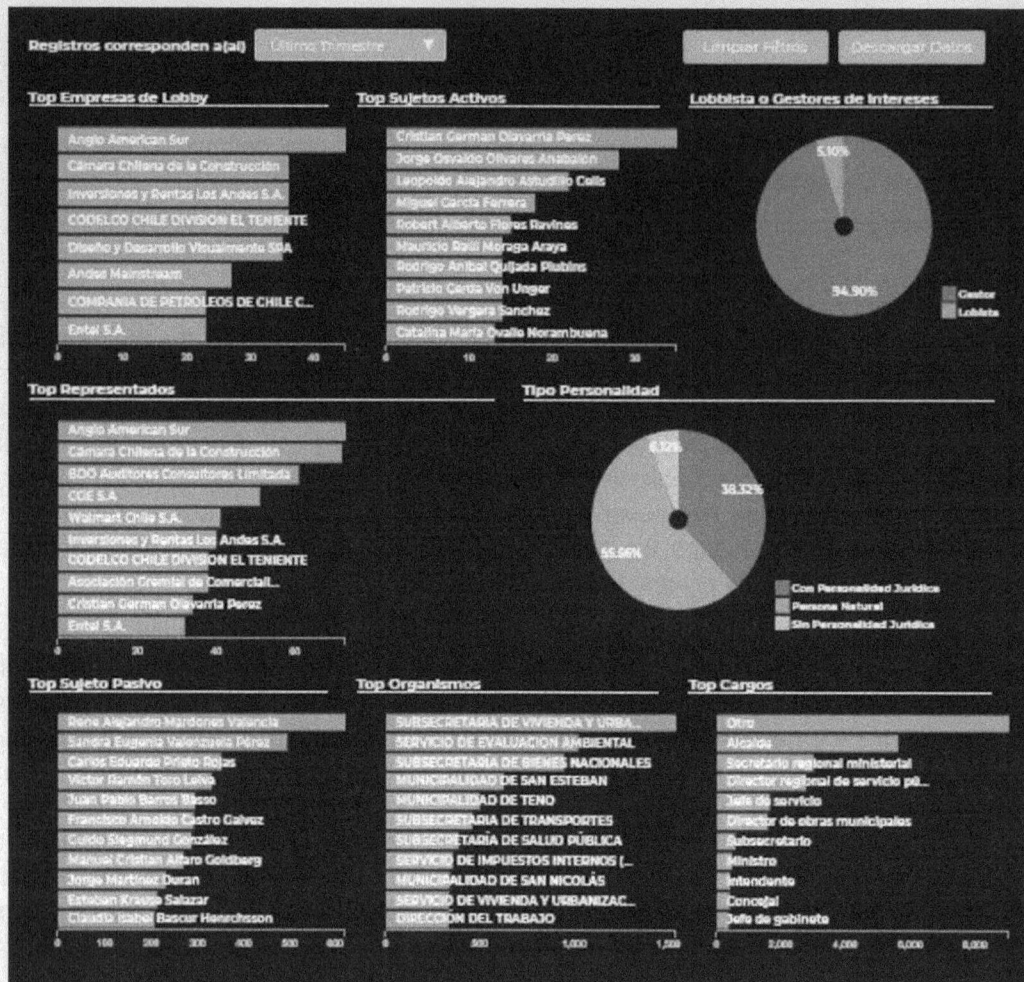

All the information can be searched and filtered by policy maker, stakeholder, or date, and it is possible to download the datasets to go through and/or reuse the data collected by the Council. Moreover, the online tool allows users to visualise time trends, compare information according to ministries and see infographics on companies, types of interest, etc.

Source: Consejo para la Transparencia, InfoLobby (n.d.), https://www.infolobby.cl/#!/busqueda-simple (accessed 19 March 2020).

However, in Thailand there are no regulations or guidelines that require or suggest that public officials involved in regulatory processes make their agendas available to the public. In this regard, and taking the opportunity of current discussions on amending the *Official Information Act B.E 2540* (1997), the Thai Government could consider including such a disposition in the new draft. Additionally, a similar requirement could be discussed in the Ethics Committee of the House of Representatives and included in the rules of procedure or the future code of conduct for parliamentarians.

Thailand could consider increasing the level of transparency with respect to the composition and activities of advisory bodies in the executive and legislative branches

Many governments establish and use advisory groups, such as committees, boards, or commissions, to inform public decision making through the provision of specific advice, expertise and recommendations. These groups are made up of public and/or private sector members and/or representatives from civil society, and may be created by the executive, legislative or judicial branches of government or government subdivisions.

Despite their relevance in decision making, there are not many regulations on these advisory bodies in OECD countries. Most OECD countries make members of advisory bodies public (Figure 3.7), but there are only a few countries that establish specific requirements for their composition, or that require members to disclose their interests. For instance, only 20% of lobbyists state that they have to disclose their interests and activities if they are part of an advisory board (2020 OECD Survey on Lobbying). In fact, the capture of these advisory groups by private interests to exert influence has been identified as an emerging risk to the integrity of policy making. When, for example, corporate executives advise governments as members of an advisory group, they act not as external lobbyists or stakeholders, but as part of the policy-making process with direct access to decision makers (OECD, 2014[10]).

Figure 3.7. In most OECD countries members of advisory bodies are known to public

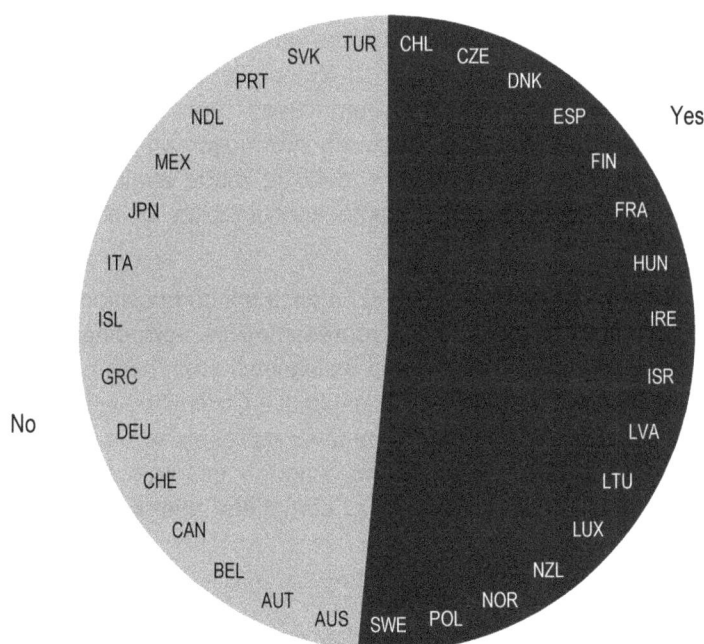

Source: OECD PMRI 2018.

In Thailand, various advisory bodies are established within the executive to support, advise and inform ministries and governmental agencies. They vary in objective, scope and functioning. There are institutionalised, long-term bodies, such as the Joint Public and Private Sector Consultative Committee (composed of senior public officials responsible for economic affairs, and private representatives, such as the Thai Chamber of Commerce, the Federation of Thai Industries, and Thai Bankers Association), and other more informal and ad-hoc entities, such as the sub-committees within the National Research Council. The members of these advisory bodies are generally appointed by the government.

Additionally, both the House of Representatives and the Senate have the power to establish 'ad hoc committees' when they deem it reasonable and necessary to address parliamentary affairs that are not under the scope of any particular standing committee, or overlap with the powers and duties of multiple standing committees. Concerning appointments to these committees, the National Constitution (Section 128) states that if a bill concerns certain social groups (children, youth, women, elderly, disabled or handicapped), one third of the committee must comprise either people belonging to the social group concerned by the bill, or representatives from private organisations who deal with this social group. Similarly, if a bill is introduced through a petition, the appointment rules of ad hoc committees stipulate a quota requiring one third of the committee to consist of representatives of people who signed the petition.

Despite their varied relevance and duration in the Thai institutional framework, these advisory bodies in the executive and legislative branches are key in decision making, and should therefore be subject to high standards of transparency and integrity. However, the OECD fact-finding mission to Thailand found that the information pertaining to members of these different committees is not available to the public, and neither are the reports on assessment evaluations, minutes of meetings, or transcripts of discussions that were held. These elements may impact on the performance of the advisory bodies, undermining their expertise and advice, affecting the transparency of decision-making processes, and increasing capture risks.

Hence, the government of Thailand could develop strict and clear regulations regarding its advisory bodies and establish transparency criteria for their composition and advice provided to policy makers. For instance, these rules could extend the scope of some related dispositions of the National Constitution in order to make it applicable to all government committees within the Executive branch. Section 129 of the National Constitution requires the Legislative branch to include in its Rules of Procedure that ad-hoc committees should disclose minutes of sittings or committees' reports, findings and studies. Therefore, and similar to most OECD countries (Figure 3.7 above), information on members of committees, as well as all relevant documents, minutes or agendas, should be made available to the public. This could strengthen transparency in decision making, promote accountability of advisory groups, and diminish capture risks.

Additional measures could include the requirement to balance the composition of advisory boards in terms of private stakeholders' participation, by including representatives from different sectors, organisations, etc. For example, only representatives from big and well-known chambers or associations are invited to participate in the Joint Public and Private Sector Consultative Committee at the national level. However, even if advisory boards include local experts or local-level representatives, there is no guarantee that a plurality of interests are represented in discussions. Another example of a measure Thailand could consider is an outright ban on industry payments to committee members, a proposal currently being discussed in Switzerland.

Strengthening enforcement and stakeholder engagement awareness raising

In order to make a stronger impact and achieve real outcomes, a comprehensive legislative framework to promote transparency and integrity in public decision making needs to be complemented by measures to raise awareness about the available information and the existing engagement mechanisms. In addition, the framework needs to be enforced to ensure that public officials respect these mechanisms, and that rules and regulations are implemented and complied with.

Thailand could further its efforts to centralise and systematise all information (including statistical data) concerning public consultations by developing a single platform

The Public Consultation Advisory Committee in Thailand, which includes government representatives and qualified persons appointed by the Council of Ministers, monitors and provides feedback on public consultations held in the country. According to the *Act on Legislative Drafting and Evaluation of Legislation B.E. 2560* (2019), once a public consultation has been held, the State agency in charge of the process has to consider the inputs for further drafting and has to enumerate at least the general topics and opinions including the reasoning provided by each participant of the public consultation. Further, the State agency has to provide, publish and present an impact assessment report. The Office of the Council of State can require the stakeholder engagement to be conducted again if needed, or inform the relevant government agency to do so.

As mentioned above, the Council of State is currently developing a single platform that will centralise and organise all information related to different public consultations. However, until now this information is still being disaggregated by State agencies, and hence there are no overall statistics or data on public consultations held in the country. The lack of centralised and co-ordinated data may undermine the best practice principle on performance assessment (OECD, 2014[11]) as well as hinder access to this information by the general public.

Many OECD countries compile and analyse information regarding stakeholder engagement processes. They collect information and produce statistics on participants of consultations (that is the case in Canada, France, Greece, among others), publish reports on the performance of consultation practices related to draft regulations (such as in Estonia, Switzerland or the United Kingdom), or even develop indicators on the functioning of consultations (in Japan, Slovenia or Mexico, among others) (OECD, 2018[7]).

In this sense, the Thai government's initiative to systematise all information concerning public consultations and make it available to the public should be continued and could be furthered by the development, compilation and analysis of statistical data. Some OECD countries' websites provide suitable examples (Box 3.6). This would allow for the identification of trends, weaknesses and comparative analysis regarding issues, agencies and mechanisms. It could even allow the government and many stakeholders to assess the impact of their engagement on different regulations and foster trust in government.

Box 3.6. Single platforms containing information on consultations

The *Consulting with Canadians* website centralises and presents all data on public consultations. Users of the platform can filter and sort information by subject, status, entities or key words. Furthermore, the website provides access to all records, and presents data in a systematised and downloadable user-friendly format.

The UK government website includes a section on Public Consultations held by government entities, presenting information about openings, and listing all public consultations that have been or are due to be held in the country. Information can be sorted by date, topic, or sub-topic.

In a similar vein, the statistics website of the government of New Zealand, *StatsNZ,* gathers all the information on public consultations carried out in the country. The data is organised by date, though users can also filter information by topic.

Source: https://www.canada.ca/en/government/system/consultations/consultingcanadians.html; https://www.gov.uk/; https://www.stats.govt.nz/consultations/?sort=5.

Thailand may develop awareness-raising campaigns and communication efforts to strengthen citizens' rights to introduce legislation

In addition to engaging stakeholders during decision-making processes and allowing citizens to provide their inputs on different initiatives, governments sometimes grant their citizens the right to propose initiatives and hence to proactively engage in shaping the public agenda. This is the case in the majority of OECD countries, which provide citizens with the possibility to present draft initiatives of legislative bills (2020 OECD Survey on Lobbying).

In Thailand, since 1997, a number of eligible voters have been granted the right to introduce bills directly to the National Assembly. The proposed bill must be related to the rights and liberties of people, or fundamental State policies, and requires the support of at least 10 000 citizens.

However, during the OECD fact-finding mission, the Office of the Council highlighted that after more than ten years of implementation, bills initiated by the electorate have proven to be impractical as a method of introducing draft laws, since they rarely pass the National Assembly due to a lack of technical and political support from the government. Public officials mentioned that only ten draft bills have been presented by citizens' initiatives. None of these have ever been successful though, for various reasons, including for example technical problems regarding the fact that bills must be related to and do not contradict any other pre-existing laws.

In this regard, the government of Thailand could consider implementing awareness-raising and communication efforts in order to make citizens more mindful of the requirements that need to be fulfilled in order to introduce legislation, and develop their capabilities to proactively engage in policy making. This could serve the purpose of both educating people on the role of Parliament, as well as encouraging them to participate in legislative processes. Current programs and campaigns carried out in some OECD member and non-member countries could be used as guidance (Box 3.7).

Box 3.7. Awareness-raising programs and campaigns

There are many ways and channels to develop awareness-raising initiatives. They may include more traditional methods such as printed flyers and posters, or online advertisements, social media campaigns, and interactive videos. Further, these initiatives can be promoted by the government itself, or through joint efforts with civil society organisations.

For instance, the UK Parliament runs the annual Parliament Week. It engages citizens from across the UK in order to discuss democracy, and citizen power, and encourages them to get involved. People who sign up receive a kit packed with goodies including an activity booklet, bunting, and a ballot box among others. They may be grouped by age and interests, and take part in many different activities, including:

- Q&A sessions, quizzes and lively debates
- creating petitions and campaigning for change
- making videos and posting online
- debating issues and holding votes
- themed assemblies and school council elections
- baking, crafting and colouring
- visits from MPs, Members of the House of Lords, local councillors or mayors, MSs, MLAs and MSPs.

Further, the program also includes a competition for a Parliament Award, and people can sign up to be included in the program mailing list to receive all information related to the initiative. In 2019, over 1.2 million people were part of the event.

Source: (ParlAmericas, n.d.[12]), Toolkit: Citizen Participation in the Legislative Process, https://www.ukparliamentweek.org/en/.

Additionally, the Thai government may consider developing an initiative that provides direct incentives for citizens to proactively engage in public life, similar to the European Citizens Initiative in the EU (Box 3.8).

Box 3.8. European Citizens Initiative

In 2011, the EU developed the European Citizens Initiative (ECI). This initiative encourages civic society participation by (1) making information on the many initiatives citizens pursue available to be presented and discussed in Parliament, and (2) facilitating connections between initiatives' supporters within different countries.

The ECI allows the European Commission to consider proposals for legislation on issues that have the signatures of at least a million EU citizens. In order to register an initiative, at least 7 EU citizens living in 7 different EU countries have to team up to support an issue. The ECI offers help by granting access to a database of registered users of the website.

Once an initiative is accepted, the Commission translates the initiative into all official languages, and then allows twelve months for the initiative to collect one million signatures. Next, these statements of support have to be validated and within the following three months, the initiative must be submitted to the Commission (together with the information on the support and funding received).

Until March 2020, there have been 96 registration requests, 72 initiatives registered and 5 successful initiatives.

Source: European Union (2020), "European Citizens' Initiative Week", https://europa.eu/citizens-initiative/_en (accessed on 23 March 2020).

Proposals for action

The analysis of the Kingdom of Thailand's policies aimed at promoting transparency and integrity in public decision making has shown that the country's legislative framework on the issue is incipient. In addition, there are practical concerns related to the enforcement and implementation of the regulations in place. The proposed reforms required to improve the quality of the framework and introduce a more coherent approach to promote transparency and integrity in decision making can be summarised as follows:

Fostering regulations on stakeholder engagement and participation in policy making

- Thailand could initiate discussions and work on developing specific rules or guidelines to regulate interactions between different stakeholders and public officials during policy making. Alternatively, it could include a directive in the Code of Professional Ethics for the Civil Service or provide a set of rules or principles establishing how public officials and policy makers must be contacted by or interact with private stakeholders. For instance, the current drafting of the Code of Conduct for Parliamentarians could be an opportunity to include these dispositions.

- The government of Thailand could use the discussions on the new Public Consultation Act to consider including specific guidelines on the processes, methods and timeframes of public consultations. Further, it would benefit from a centralised system to organise consultations such as the planned online platform currently in development, to provide stakeholders with all relevant information on engagement processes.

Promoting transparency and access to information on decision making

- Thailand could take advantage of current discussions on the *Official Information Act B.E 2540* (1997) reform to include dispositions that could guide citizens requesting public information. Besides, and in order to ensure effective implementation of the legislative framework, the government of Thailand could strengthen and further promote the independence of Thailand's Information Commissioner by creating specific requirements for the Commissioner's appointment and assigning an independent budget to the post.

- Further, in order to foster citizens' trust in government, It would be key for the government to provide complete information throughout the different legislative stages, and gear the information towards promoting transparency in decision-making processes. The ongoing development of a platform including this information will be extremely beneficial in this regard. Meanwhile, as an initial step, the National Assembly website could be updated in order to systematise all available information and provide a more user-friendly platform.

- Within the context of the current discussions on amending the *Official Information Act B.E 2540* (1997), the government of Thailand could also consider including a disposition or guideline that would require or suggest that public officials involved in regulatory processes make their agendas available to the public. A similar requirement could be discussed for the House of Representatives and included in the rules of procedure or the future code of conduct for parliamentarians.

- Thailand could consider extending provisions of Section 129 of the National Constitution to most government committees within the Executive branch. Hence, information on members of committees would become available to the public, as well as all the relevant documents, minutes or agendas. Additional measures could include the requirement to ensure balance with respect to the composition of advisory boards in terms of private stakeholders' participation, or implement a ban on industry payments to committee members.

Strengthening enforcement and stakeholder engagement awareness raising

- Thailand could further its efforts to centralise and systematise all information concerning public consultations by developing a single platform including statistical data, which would allow for the identification of trends and weaknesses, and comparative analysis of issues, agencies and mechanisms.

- The government of Thailand could consider implementing awareness-raising and communications initiatives to make citizens more mindful of the requirements that need to be fulfilled in order to initiate legislation, and develop their capabilities to proactively engage in policy making.

References

Berg, J. and D. Freund (2015), *EU LEGISLATIVE FOOTPRINT: What´s the real influence of lobbying?*, Transparency International-EU Office, Brussels, https://transparency.eu/wp-content/uploads/2016/09/Transparency-05-small-text-web-1.pdf. [9]

Nimitmongkol, M. (2019), *Why is corruption not reduced?*, ACT, Anti-Corruption Organization of Thailand, http://www.anticorruption.in.th/2016/en/detail/1427/1/%E0%B8%97%E0%B8%B3%E0%B9%84%E0%B8%A1%E0%B8%84%E0%B8%AD%E0%B8%A3%E0%B9%8C%E0%B8%A3%E0%B8%B1%E0%B8%9B%E0%B8%8A%E0%B8%B1%E0%B8%99%E0%B9%84%E0%B8%A1%E0%B9%88%E0%B8%A5%E0%B8%94%E0%B8%A5%E0%B8%87%20? (accessed on 12 August 2020). [6]

OECD (2019), *Multi-dimensional Review of Thailand: Volume 3: From Analysis to Action*, OECD Development Pathways, OECD Publishing, Paris, https://dx.doi.org/10.1787/7ef9363b-en. [4]

OECD (2018), *OECD Integrity Review of Thailand: Towards Coherent and Effective Integrity Policies*, OECD Public Governance Reviews, OECD Publishing, Paris, https://dx.doi.org/10.1787/9789264291928-en. [5]

OECD (2018), *OECD Regulatory Policy Outlook 2018*, OECD Publishing, Paris, https://doi.org/10.1787/9789264303072-en. [7]

OECD (2017), *OECD Recommendation of the Council on Public Integrity*, OECD, Paris, http://www.oecd.org/gov/ethics/OECD-Recommendation-Public-Integrity.pdf. [3]

OECD (2017), *Preventing Policy Capture: Integrity in Public Decision Making*, OECD Public Governance Reviews, OECD Publishing, Paris, https://dx.doi.org/10.1787/9789264065239-en. [2]

OECD (2017), *Trust and Public Policy: How Better Governance Can Help Rebuild Public Trust,*, OECD Publishing, Paris, https://doi.org/10.1787/9789264268920-en. [1]

OECD (2014), *Lobbyists, Governments and Public Trust, Volume 3: Implementing the OECD Principles for Transparency and Integrity in Lobbying*, OECD Publishing, Paris, https://dx.doi.org/10.1787/9789264214224-en. [10]

OECD (2014), *The Governance of Regulators*, OECD Best Practice Principles for Regulatory Policy, OECD Publishing, Paris, https://dx.doi.org/10.1787/9789264209015-en. [11]

Ongkittikul, S. and N. Thongphat (2016), "Regulatory Coherence: The Case of Thailand", in Gill, D. and P. Intal (eds.), *The Development of Regulatory Management Systems in East Asia: Country Studies- ERIA Research Project Report 2014-5*, ERIA, Jakarta. [8]

ParlAmericas (n.d.), *Toolkit: Citizen Participation in the Legislative Process*, http://parlamericas.org/uploads/documents/Toolkit_Citizen%20Participation%20in%20the%20Legislative%20Process.pdf. [12]